VANESSA HOLBURN

Vanessa is an author and journalist with over 30 years of industry experience across consumer and trade press, digital media and communication agencies.

This is Vanessa's sixth non-fiction book. Her titles typically cover historical and modern day political and feminist topics, and she was recently part of a law-changing campaign that took her to Number 10. Vanessa's written work has appeared in national newspapers including *The Telegraph*, *The Daily Express*, *The Mirror* and *The Sun*, and in magazines such as *Private Eye*, *Fabulous*, *Bella*, *Woman's Own*, *The Jewish Chronicle*, *Yours*, *Dogs Today*, *Ask The Doctor* and *Running Fitness*. She has appeared on radio and television, and spoken on podcasts and at literary festivals, libraries, universities and museums.

Vanessa lives in Berkshire with her family and a trio of rescue pets.

First published in the UK in 2025 by River Light Press, an imprint of Aurora Metro Publications Ltd. 80 Hill Rise, Richmond, TW10 6UB, UK.
www.riverlightpress.com   X: @riverlightpress
FB: AuroraMetroBooks   Instagram: @aurora_metro
X: @aurorametro

Secret Women: What We Hide and Why © Copyright 2025 Vanessa Holburn
Editors: Mark Gunn and Sally Mears
Cover design © Copyright 2025 Aurora Metro Publications Ltd.

All rights are strictly reserved. For rights enquiries contact the publisher: info@riverlightpress.com

We are grateful to the interviewees who have given permission for their interviews to be published in this book. Some names have been changed for the protection of the contributors.

No part of this publication may be reproduced, stored in or introduced into a retrieval system, or transmitted in any form, or by any means (electronic, mechanical, photocopying, recording or otherwise) without the prior permission of the publisher. Any person who does any unauthorised act in relation to this publication may be liable to criminal prosecution and civil claims for damages. The publisher prohibits use of the work for purposes of training artificial intelligence technologies to generate text, including without limitation, technologies that are capable of generating works in the same style or genre as the work, without the prior permission of the publisher. In accordance with Article 43(3) of the DSM Directive 2019/790 the publisher expressly reserves this work from the text and data mining exception.

This book is sold subject to the condition that it shall not, by way of trade or otherwise, be lent, resold, hired out, or otherwise circulated without the publisher's prior consent in any form other than that in which it is published and without a similar condition being imposed on the subsequent purchaser.

Printed on sustainably resourced paper.

ISBNs: 978-1-0684674-0-0 (print)
978-1-0684674-3-1 (ebook)

Typeset using Atomik ePublisher from Easypress Technologies.

SECRET WOMEN

What We Hide and Why

by

VANESSA HOLBURN

RIVER LIGHT PRESS

*This book is dedicated to all the women I had the privilege
to speak to during the book's creation.
Thank you.*

ACKNOWLEDGMENTS

Of course, finding people to talk to when you're writing a book about secrets is not the easiest thing to do! As well as the women who came forward to speak to me from social media and real-life call outs, I'd like to thank the army of people who helped put me in touch with some of the interviewees.

These include Shabnam Nasimi, co-founder and director of the Friends of Afghan Women Network, PR guru Karin Ridgers, Debbie Wilson of the IAWPC, Katie White of Enough, Laura London, chair of The Magic Circle Council, Dr Mary Wakeham of Refuge4Pets, Beverley Cuddy Editor of *Dogs Today* magazine, author and journalist CJ DeBarra, friends Yonni and Marnie, neighbour Victoria, fellow members of the Society of Authors WhatsApp group for non-fiction writers, Hetty, Lucinda and Andrea, and Charlotte Crisp for her fantastic Lightbulb group on Facebook. Apologies in advance if I've forgotten anyone. I have kept a couple of names secret here too!

And finally, a big thank you to Lucy Melville of River Light Press for trusting me with the initial inspiration behind the book and offering both contacts and support along the way.

CONTENTS

Introduction	vii

SECTION 1: ACTIVISM AND CAMPAIGNS
Chapter 1: The Afghan Rebels	15
Chapter 2: Voices for the Animals	25
Chapter 3: Child Sexual Abuse and Domestic Abuse Campaigners	35
Chapter 4: The Sexual Assault Survivor	53

SECTION 2: WORK AND SELF-DEVELOPMENT
Chapter 5: Wartime Bombe Operator	63
Chapter 6: Private Investigators and Mystery Shopping	71
Chapter 7: The Magic Circle and Freemasonry	79
Chapter 8: Adult Content and the Professional Mistress	89

SECTION 3: PERSONAL RELATIONSHIPS
Chapter 9: Lesbian Lives	103
Chapter 10: Secret Love Affairs	113
Chapter 11: Kink and Fetish Relationships	125
Chapter 12: Hypersexuality as a result of Incest	135

SECTION 4: BEING YOURSELF
Chapter 13: Witchcraft and the Occult	149
Chapter 14: Neo-Shamanism	157
Chapter 15: ADHD and Mental Health	165
Chapter 16: Weight-loss Jabs	183

Conclusion	195
Further resources	201

INTRODUCTION

secret

noun
a piece of information that is only known by a single person
or a select few and should not be shared with others:

adjective
if something is secret, other people are
not allowed to know about it:
used to refer to a person's particular habit, hobby or feeling
that they do not tell or show other people:

We all keep secrets at some point in our lives, and we're all interested in the secrets that other people are keeping too. But secrets can be dangerous, to ourselves and to others. They can protect but they can harm.

In this book, women who are very different in age, race, culture, lifestyle and geographical location share their secrets with us. They cover both things that they choose to do in private, and things that have happened to them, with and without their consent. They are secrets that they keep so that they can live, work, learn and grow. Some of the stories shared are sad, some are sexy. Many are inspirational, a few dispiriting. They have been hidden to protect their owner and others.

For some, this is the first time they have spoken to anyone about what they have chosen to keep close and confidential. For other women, while they are now openly campaigning and talking about their experiences and beliefs, they kept their secrets hidden in the past, often for decades. Some of those I spoke to may have a public face but need to do some of their work undercover and keep it private.

Here, they all share their secrets for the good of others because someone out there might be experiencing something similar. And whatever the secret, there is common ground. In sharing what they keep, or have kept, a secret, they can help us to understand why.

We often think of secrets as feminine in nature and we perhaps like to portray women as the more secretive sex, whispering behind raised hands and exchanging knowing looks. We belittle women's chatter about secrets, calling it gossip and tittle tattle, call women mean girls when they write a diary for their eyes only. How often is the village gossip in a novel characterised as a woman?

In contrast, we are taught to trust men with our secrets; they are the doctor in a consulting room or the priest in the confessional; respected and professional. Men with secrets are strong and silent; daring spies refusing to tell our enemies however much they are tortured.

I too fell for this cliché of the secretive female. Before I spoke to these women and sat down to write this book, I thought the content would be thrilling and possibly titillating, fun stories and scandalous secrets, clandestine meetings and salacious sex clubs. And while some of the women I've spoken to do discuss the joy of secrets past and present, it's more often about vulnerable women having to keep their own secrets and the secrets of other women for safety and to avoid judgement.

Some of what we women keep secret seems to be a result of not fulfilling the roles forced upon us when it comes to personality, profession, interests, desires or sexuality, or because our passions are considered 'female-only' interests, including intuitive beliefs and practices such as witchcraft – meaning they must be of less importance or given less credence.

But the stories within these chapters offer so much.

Even with decades of journalistic experience behind me, and several years writing books and features that specifically focus on the personal and professional lives of women, the accounts were, at times, incredibly moving. They brought me to tears.

You'll find the book divided into sections: Activism and Campaigns, Work and Self-development, Personal Relationships and Being Yourself. It wasn't easy to categorise these women and their secrets, many bleed across the divisions and defy such an artificial and manmade definition.

Within the first section, Activism and Campaigns, we meet some incredibly brave women. First, we talk to Afghan rebels Roya and Safia, who at great risk to their personal safety, defy the oppressive regime that every day intensifies its war on women and its desire to erase women from public life completely. We also speak to Latifa in Morocco and Juliet in the UK about how they work, sometimes in secret, to protect those that do not have a voice and to educate the public about animal welfare conditions across the world. We meet Emma-Jane and Sam, who have endured cruelty and coercion through child sexual abuse and domestic abuse, but rose above their abusers and now campaign to raise awareness and demand systemic change to prevent the same thing happening to other women and girls. Finally, we speak to Ella about her experience with sexual assault discussing how silence did and did not serve her, and why she now chooses to speak up about what happened to her. All these women are living, or have lived through or witnessed, trauma, but they continue to fight for what is right.

The next section, Work and Self-development, features women whose professional roles and growth require secrecy in one way or another. This includes the story of Barbara, who was a wartime Bombe operator in the Eastcote outstation of Bletchley Park, and signed the Official Secrets Act in her late teens. Barbara did not speak about her work at Eastcote until she was in her 80s and official wartime files had been declassified. We also meet Jen and Sarah who both work as private investigators (while Jen had a previous, rather fun, life as a mystery shopper) and detail how they work undercover and deal with the confidentiality and discretion their roles require. Personal safety is similarly an issue in the lives of these women as they seek justice on behalf of others.

Next, we discuss the mystery that surrounds the performance of magic with Laura, chair of industry society The Magic Circle Council. She explains the power of secret knowledge and what makes that so special. We also speak to two female Freemasons, Viviane and Susan, based in America. They open up on why they joined the organisation, how they benefit from it and why it is not the male-only secret society popular culture would have us believe. Roxy, an adult content provider from the States discusses how she keeps her very different lives separate and safe, and why there's a security-coded lock on her bedroom door. We meet Madam Mayhem whose adult work has helped her work through the limiting beliefs she grew up with surrounding women and their sexual pleasure. Finally, we speak to Rebecca, a professional mistress and dominatrix about how her work means she is a keeper of secrets.

Our third section deals with love and lust and everything in between under the umbrella of personal relationships. How do you have a relationship in secret and what if that affair is frowned upon by those around you or society at large, or even something you yourself can't accept? We talk to Maureen and Norah about coming out later in life, and how denying their true sexual identities prevented them from living life to the full, left them isolated and fed addiction. We also hear from Helen, who was sad to discover her mother had spent a lifetime denying her sexuality. We speak to Diana and Sophie about their extra-marital affairs then and now, how and why they happened, and why they don't regret their romantic dalliances in the slightest. We also meet Maryam who is keeping her dating life secret from her father. Sarah from Spain talks to us about her former life as a submissive in a BDSM relationship, deftly putting *Fifty Shades* to shame. We talk to Melissa whose throuple experience didn't go to plan. Finally, we meet Bea, who is a survivor of incest and experienced the most terrible treatment at the hands of her own father. She teaches us about hypersexuality, or sexual addiction, and how she needed society to support not shame her to recover. Bea's story in particular is a wake-up call to our judicial system that continues to fail its female survivors.

The last section in the book covers beliefs, mental health and our physical selves. These are the things that make us, us. We might choose them, and we might not, and of course, either way society has something to say about that! Here Lily and Esme explain how they classify themselves as a baby witch and a hedge witch respectively, and why pointy hats and covens have nothing to do with how they practice witchcraft and related arts. We discuss the study of the occult and why silence is golden within that, with Soror D.P.B.O., who uses her magical motto to identify herself. We talk to Patricia who must combine her neo-Shamanic skills and beliefs with her conventional church role discreetly to avoid unnecessary confrontation and possible excommunication. From there we move onto neurodiversity and mental health.

CJ tells us about their journey to accepting their ADHD diagnosis, and how advocating for what they need, rather than hiding it, makes life so much easier. We speak to Emma, who has recently received an ADHD diagnosis and is coming to terms with accepting and being more open about it and her mental health challenges, in part so that she can be the best parent to her own daughters. We talk to Jenny about her reticence to discuss her ADHD diagnosis, because of societal ennui and a desire not to overshadow her son's neurodiversity. Finally, our last three women talk about their secret use of weight-loss jabs and how everybody has an opinion on a medication which has changed their lives. Joanna, Margaret and Louise have felt shamed for being overweight in the past but have found stepping away from the stigma attached to using GLP-1 is no easier.

I hope reading this book will make you smile at times, perhaps it will also make you cry.

All the stories are written as they have been told to me, in the voices of each of the 'Secret Women'.

If you are affected by any of the issues discussed, please find a further resources section at the end of the book, organised by chapter.

There are also pages left blank at the end of the book and we encourage you to make your own notes or record your own thoughts and a 'secret diary' of your own.

Many of the women featured in the book have used aliases to protect their identity; to further protect them we have not indicated which women they are. This enables our Secret Women to talk freely.

SECTION 1

ACTIVISM AND CAMPAIGNS

CHAPTER 1

The Afghan Rebels

'I can say without exaggeration that I spend every single moment in fear. The danger is constant.'

Roya is from Afghanistan and works in secret against the Taliban regime that took power in 2021 after US and international forces left the country. The Taliban, which enforced Islamic rule following a devastating civil war, had previously been ousted by a US-led invasion in 2001. Today the Taliban government is not formally recognised by any other country and imposes strict Sharia law on the people of Afghanistan, including severe restrictions on women and girls. In September 2025, the Taliban shutdown internet and telecommunications services across the country for 48 hours, citing a decree by their leader, Hibatullah Akhundzada, aimed at curbing 'immorality'.

I'm communicating with Roya via an app that uses end-to-end encryption to secure all communications. She is part of a small network of women quietly, but determinedly, working against the Taliban. As such she must protect herself and her family from scrutiny in each and every way she can.

'Before, Afghan women were active in many fields, social, political, economic, and educational. They held government positions, worked in organisations, and contributed meaningfully to society. However, once the Taliban took control, all these freedoms were taken away. Women were banned from education, work and public spaces. Universities and schools were closed for girls, women were no longer allowed to work in most institutions, and even going outside the home without a male guardian became dangerous or impossible.'

Afghan leaders have effectively erased Afghan women from public life and restricted their movement. In December 2024 the media reported that Afghanistan's Supreme Leader, Hibatullah Akhundzada, had issued an order banning the construction of windows in residential buildings that overlook areas used by women and said that existing ones should be blocked.[1] The United Nations (UN) reports that the multitude of restrictions make access to reproductive rights, maternal health care, education and mental health services difficult and warns that Afghan women are increasingly isolated.[2]

On August 15th, 2025, to mark the fourth anniversary of the Taliban's return to power, the UK Committee for UN Women, the UN agency for gender equality and women's empowerment, shared sobering statistics across its social media platform. It said that girls in Afghanistan are banned from attending school after primary level, that 78 per cent of young Afghan women are not in education, employment or training and that only 38 per cent of women there feel they can influence decisions made in their own households. It also said that less than seven per cent of Afghan women have a bank account, that by 2026 early childbearing is projected to rise by 45 per cent and that maternal mortality could increase by more than 50 per cent.

At first Roya tells me there was a short period of 'relative flexibility' when the Taliban took control. Some schools reopened, women went back to certain jobs, and a few universities accepted female students. But this didn't last.

'Over time, strict and harsh decrees began to target women specifically. The 'Ministry of Vice and Virtue' issued orders that deeply affected every aspect of women's lives. Institutions responsible for protecting women's rights, such as the Ministry of Women's Affairs, special courts for addressing violence against women, and related judicial bodies, were dissolved. As a result, legal and social problems for women began to rise rapidly.'

Roya describes how after the Taliban banned women from education and work, and closed universities and schools she came together with like-minded women she had known either professionally or personally to work against the regime.

'We came together to resist,' she says.

'Our activism began in December 2022, in secret gatherings, offering legal and psychological support for women, and underground education for girls. Even under oppression, we raise our voices for Afghan women's rights.

'We also established a legal support committee composed of female lawyers, judges, and former prosecutors who provide legal advice and support to women facing legal challenges. Additionally, we included professionals with backgrounds in psychology to help women suffering from trauma, anxiety, and depression due to the crisis.'

UN Women agrees that the confinement to the home that Afghan women face has significant mental health implications, limiting women's access to physical exercise, social networks and communities, and adequate hygiene and sanitation facilities. It says there is 'an acute mental health crisis, particularly among women and girls, whose distressing situation has given rise to a sense of hopelessness, anxiety, and despair[2].'

'One of our most important activities is our secret educational program for girls who are now banned from going to school. We organise home-based classes in subjects like mathematics, chemistry, and physics. These efforts aim to build their knowledge, confidence, and resilience, so they are not left behind.'

'Despite all these limitations, we did not remain silent. A number of Afghan women, including myself, gathered secretly to continue our activism. We created small groups and held private meetings to share updates and document human rights violations. We worked with organisations such as UN Women to report these abuses and find possible solutions for Afghan women.'

Because of the restrictions and surveillance, any woman working in secret against the regime is in danger, and trusting others, even other women, is not easy. This makes forming any sort of resistance far harder.

'Those of us who are now working together already knew each other from before. We shared similar concerns. However, when the Taliban returned to power, everything changed. Out of fear, we all became isolated. We were scared that if our identities or past activities were revealed, we would be in danger. We even hid from our closest friends, afraid that any connection might put us at risk.'

'At first, we were scattered, silent, and uncertain. But over time, little by little, we started to reconnect. Quiet conversations turned into meaningful discussions. We began to share ideas and hopes, and eventually, we realised that we couldn't just sit and watch our rights be erased. That's when we decided to come together and act, quietly, carefully, and with full awareness of the risks.'

'Our group remains small and discreet because we still struggle with trust. We cannot easily include new people, as there's always a risk that our activities might be exposed. So, we stay limited in numbers and focus on building strong internal trust. What brought us together – and kept us together – was our shared purpose.'

In a show of female strength and unity, the rebel women now work together to help the women and girls of their country. In October 2021, the Centre for Information Resilience (CIR) launched Afghan Witness to collect, preserve and verify information on human rights and security. It supplies this information to international organisations, policymakers and the media to raise awareness of the reality of everyday life for Afghans living in the country. Afghan Witness says there is a sharp increase in gender-based violence as well as forced and early marriage. It reports that between January 2022 and June 2024, Afghan Witness recorded

840 incidents of gender-based violence against women and girls, including 332 killings.[3]

'We all agreed on the same values and goals. Our main objective was to create something better: a future where Afghan women are recognised as valuable, where their rights are respected, and where no woman has to stay silent again. Once we aligned our vision and trusted each other, we began to organise and work in harmony.'

'It took time and patience, but eventually, we became united. Our work now is built on a foundation of mutual trust, shared values, and a deep belief that Afghan women deserve better – and that change is still possible.'

Roya describes the current experience of the women of her homeland as 'one of the darkest periods in our history'. Many of the women already working in human and women's rights sought asylum elsewhere, another reason why the tight-knit group of female activists remains small.

'We are not a large group, and we cannot easily expand. The lack of trust and serious security concerns prevent us from adding new members. For our safety, we prefer to keep the group as it is, small, trusted, and committed. We work together based on shared goals that are driven by our lived experiences and personal convictions. '

'At this point, we are just a few women who have come together, and we operate only at a local level. We cannot work on a national scale because we have no direct connection or familiarity with women in other provinces. So, for now, we focus on our local circle, on the women we know and trust, and we continue our activities in this limited but meaningful way.'

Roya remains hopeful of a better future, but realistic about the dangers she and her network face.

'Despite all the risks, I believe in resistance, solidarity, and hope. Through education, legal aid, mental health support, and awareness, we continue to fight for the rights and dignity of Afghan women, no matter how difficult the circumstances may be'.

The group have successfully observed days such as March 8

(International Women's Day) and November 25 (International Day for the Elimination of Violence Against Women) through posters, statements, and small online events.

'We held webinars focused on women's rights, legal awareness, and strategies for resilience under Taliban rule,' says Roya.

But Roya is never far from danger in a place where all the structures and institutions designed to work for women, such as the Ministry of Women's Affairs, have been deliberately dismantled in what Roya describes as 'systematic actions against women'.

'Life under Taliban rule is extremely dangerous, especially for women, and even more so for those of us who are still trying to speak out or resist in any way,' Roya says.

'You may have seen media reports about Afghan women who protested – many of them have been forcibly disappeared, some were tortured, some imprisoned, and others even faced sexual violence. These are not just stories; they are part of our reality.'

'We carry out our work with great caution, but that doesn't mean we are safe. I feel danger all around me. Every time I leave the house, I worry that I'm being followed. When I speak on the phone, I worry that my voice is being recorded. If I see a car stop next to me on the street, I fear it could be the Taliban, ready to kidnap or harm me. Even when I try to sleep, fear keeps me awake.

'And it's not just about me, I constantly fear for my family. I worry about my elderly father, my brother. If the Taliban find out about my activities, they won't just punish me – they will harass my family, maybe even arrest or beat them. I also worry about how my family would survive if something happened to me. Who will provide for them? Who will pay for food, shelter, or basic needs?'

'These are the risks we face every day. But despite everything, we continue – because staying silent, sitting within the four walls of our home, won't bring change. We must act, no matter how dangerous it is, because someone has to speak up for Afghan women. Someone has to remind the world that half of Afghanistan's population cannot be erased.'

But secrecy is still an essential way of life for Roya and her group, even her family don't know the truth about her activism.

'I haven't informed my family about my activities. I don't tell them because I know it would worry them deeply. My father, for example, always advises me not to get involved in things that challenge the current regime or its values'. He says, 'Don't resist them, just accept the circumstances. But I can't.'

'Whenever I have meetings or planning sessions for our work, I try to keep everything secret. I close my door tightly and schedule my activities at times when my family thinks I'm asleep or not at home. I even delete or hide my messages and documents so no one in my family accidentally discovers what I'm doing.'

'Sometimes when I leave the house, they ask many questions, 'Where are you going? Why? What are you doing?' It takes time and emotional energy to give them believable answers. It's painful. No one in my family knows about the women's rights work I'm doing, especially since it goes directly against the Taliban's ideology.'

'I keep it secret because I know they would try to stop me, not because they don't believe in justice, but because they fear for my safety and for our family. They are afraid of what could happen if I am caught. They wonder, if something happens to my family, who will take care of the family? The weight of all this is heavy. But as an Afghan girl, as a woman fighting for change, I feel I have no other choice.'

Roya is all too aware of the real and physical danger she is placing herself in, that her family are also at risk and that if she is caught her activism might come to an end.

'If I were caught by the Taliban, there are several possible outcomes and none of them are safe. I could be forcibly disappeared, imprisoned, or subjected to physical and psychological torture. The risk of sexual violence is also very real. These are not just fears, they are known tactics that have been used against other women activists in Afghanistan.'

'And it wouldn't end with me. My male family members, my

father, my brother, would also be at risk. They could be arrested, beaten, or harassed simply for being related to me. The Taliban often use family to punish and silence women.'

'If I were caught, I might never be able to return to public life again. I might lose the ability to continue my activism. I might be silenced permanently.'

'And yet, I still speak out. I have participated in peaceful protests, and I've shared my thoughts and frustrations about the Taliban on platforms like Facebook. I know these actions could be used against me. But despite the danger, I continue because I believe in the struggle for Afghan women's rights.'

Roya has been stopped and questioned by armed members of the Taliban and it's now likely that she is known to them.

'The first time [I was suspected] was during a peaceful protest in Herat that we had helped organise in support of female university students who were banned from attending school. I coordinated efforts to unite girls from different areas so we could protest together. Unfortunately, as I left my house and began walking toward the meeting point, I was stopped by a group of Taliban members. They blocked my way and refused to let me continue. When I tried to explain and protest, one of them pointed his rifle directly at my chest. It was only after people from the neighbourhood intervened that I was allowed to return home. I was shaken but not silenced.'

'The second incident happened while I was at home. I had just finished lunch when I heard unusual noises outside. From the window, I saw a large number of armed men surrounding our house. I quickly turned off my phone and hid it deep inside my pillow to avoid it being found. A few minutes later, they banged on our door, demanding entry. My sisters and I had just woken up from a nap and were terrified. When we opened the door, they stormed into our house without permission.'

'They searched everything. Luckily, I wasn't the only one at home, they took another family member with them and held her for about three to four hours. Our house was under siege the entire time.

They later accused us of having ties to the previous government and claimed I had supported women's movements and opposed the Taliban. From that moment on, our house was marked. They made it clear that my activities, and my past support for the Islamic Republic, put me at great risk.'

So, what of the future for Roya and her group, and for the women and girls in Afghanistan?

'Those who have accepted the Taliban's values and ideology, those who either stayed at home without pursuing education or activism, or who now work within the Taliban system, are generally left alone. These women have aligned themselves with the Taliban's expectations and are therefore considered 'safe' by the regime.'

'In contrast, independent women, those who are educated, outspoken, and involved in activism, are constantly at risk. They do not accept the Taliban's view of women and are seen as threats. Young Afghan girls, especially those who resist or dream of more, are not safe. Forced marriages, disappearances, and threats have happened and continue to happen. We've seen it with our own eyes. We've lived it.'

The dangerous nature of her work, and the need to operate in secret for her own safety and the safety of those she loves will not, however, deter Roya as she works against the Taliban for a better future for the females of her homeland.

'We fight because we must. Even if the world has forgotten us, we have not forgotten each other. I still hold on to hope that one day, change will come. Until then, we continue the fight, even in the shadows,' she says.

The future is what most worries **Safia**, another activist, particularly as she is mother to young girls. She has been forced out of employment in what she refers to as 'dangerous times and moments' since the Taliban took control.

'The Taliban told me that as a woman I could not be a manager in my organisation, so I had to leave and return from where I worked to the city.'

Her teenage daughter is also now forced to stay home instead of completing her education at high school and is unable even to visit friends and peers. Despite this she continues her education in secret via online lessons. Safia has watched many professional women emigrate from the country and tells her daughters that Afghanistan is 'not the place to live in comfort'.

'Young girls have a lot of problems; they are banned from school and medical services. They have challenges and barriers. They've lost all their hope and are forced to abandon their future plans.'

'We are in danger; we are afraid every day,' she says. 'It is hard for me and all of our sisters and mothers, we see the Taliban everywhere, in the streets, in offices'.

'But I gather with women and talk to them about violence, forced marriage and other things that are happening, and I record this'.

'I don't speak to my neighbours about what I do, but I do work with four or five of my close friends, meeting in our homes to speak about the situation and update each other on the news.'

References

1. https://www.france24.com/en/live-news/20241229-taliban-leader-bans-windows-overlooking-women-s-areas (accessed Sept 2025)

2. https://www.unwomen.org/en/articles/faqs/faqs-afghan-women-three-years-after-the-taliban-takeover (accessed Sept 2025)

3. https://www.amnesty.org/en/location/asia-and-the-pacific/south-asia/afghanistan/report-afghanistan/ (accessed Sept 2025)

CHAPTER 2

Voices for the Animals

'I told my husband about the abuse, and he spoke to his family, but they wouldn't help, and so I realised we were alone in caring about this issue.'

Watching her daughter suffer led **Latifa** to begin her animal activism in her adopted home of Morocco. She learnt quickly that it would be something she had to do in secret. A foreign national with Moroccan heritage, she was keen to embrace life in the country her parents grew up in. But, after her first year there, events took a turn for the worse, leaving her daughter traumatised, angry and non-communicative.

'My daughter loves animals in general, so she was always outside playing with the street dogs. One of the dogs had one leg broken and didn't walk well, she loved that dog and the dog recognised her, but a male neighbour was always making loud comments about the dog and one day took a stick and beat it'.

'A few days later I sent my daughter, who was 12 at the time, to the bin area with some rubbish, and four male workers also started to harass her about feeding this dog, and told her if she continued, they would poison the dog'.

'I told my husband about the abuse, and he spoke to his family, but they wouldn't help, and so I realised we were alone in caring about this issue.'

In 2020, the Animal Protection Index, produced by World Animal Protection, which ranks 50 countries around the world according to their animal welfare policy and legislation to support its lobbying efforts, graded Morrocco as an 'F' on a scale that ranges from 'A' to 'G'. It found that animal welfare legislation was extremely limited in Morocco and that while provisions exist regarding animal health, provisions have not been made to improve animal welfare. Animal protection in Morocco is governed by the Criminal Code, which prohibits the killing of pets and the poisoning of farm and working animals, but the emphasis is on protecting animals as property rather than on a welfare perspective, and there is no dedicated government body responsible for animal welfare.[1] In November 2019, the Moroccan government announced a new national scheme to trap-neuter-release and mass vaccinate the roaming dog population.

Latifa saw the impact that this 'F-grade' government approach creates.

'Next the police came, and another neighbour saw them take the dog. We looked for her and once saw her in the town centre, so we knew they had deliberately displaced her.'

'After that I began to feel unsafe, so fed and cared for the street dogs in secret'.

'Before long, my daughter formed a bond with another dog, a sterilised Dalmatian. This dog was respected by the neighbours as he was protecting some puppies that had been left orphaned when their mother was poisoned. People were feeding the puppies but only one survived, so we took it into our house'.

'I still received verbal abuse about the Dalmatian, neighbours commenting that I had been feeding it, perhaps people were scared of it? It was a big dog but had never bitten anyone.'

'Then at 3am one morning when I was alone in the house a noise woke me. Outside I saw vehicles, a lorry, the police and ten men, one with a rifle. They shot a dog. Then I knew I was not safe, that I was in a war zone'.

'A couple of months passed, and the authorities were coming every fortnight killing all the dogs in the neighbourhood. I couldn't sleep but I kept what was going on from my daughter to protect her.'

'Unfortunately, she was out walking our dog one day and saw the mother of a dog that had lived near us. The mother dog was lying on the ground with gunshot wounds, with puppies trying to feed from her'.

This was a pivotal point for Latifa, with the trauma of seeing the murdered dog significantly affecting her daughter.

'This was when my daughter began to change. She didn't want to take our dog out anymore; she didn't want to play with any of the street dogs anymore. Instead, she picked up my phone and buried herself in social media. I didn't see her anymore, she didn't want to sleep near me, she wanted to be alone'.

'At first, I didn't make the connection, I thought she was just being a teenager. But after a month I saw her push our dog away when it approached her, it was then I realised what she had seen had had an impact on her mental health. I also learnt that someone had told her the Dalmatian she loved had been shot'.

'The funny thing is that lots of people are animal lovers here, but those that are not, are aggressive, like a mafia. So, I told my husband that we animal lovers need to communicate, to know who we all are. And I started to do my research.'

'That's when I found out about the International Animal Coalition (IAWPC), and through it what is really happening. That the dog killings are happening on a national level by order of the authorities because of the World Cup, which means the five or ten per cent of the population that are horrible to animals now feel they can do what they like'.

The IAWPC consists of 27 respected international animal welfare and protection organisations from around the world, it comes together when issues of serious and major concern relating to the welfare and protection of animals come to its attention, often as a result of pleas for help from groups within a particular country.

It's campaigning to end the violent and inhumane mass killings of street dogs in Morocco and says that 'Almost every day, individuals acting on behalf of the Moroccan government, tour the streets shooting, poisoning and catching dogs.'[2] And that the methods used are considered inhumane management practices resulting in considerable pain, suffering and a lingering death. It also says that since FIFA made its announcement in October 2023, that Morocco would co-host the 2030 World Cup with Spain and Portugal, the barbaric killing has increased.

The IAWPC estimates that over 300,000 street and owned dogs lose their lives every year, because of Morocco's brutal killing methods, often in front of a witnessing public, including children, which is highly traumatic. And that those who protest, are intimidated and threatened.

'I got to know some people that feel like me and joined some groups that communicate via WhatsApp and Facebook' says Latifa.

'It is comforting being in the group because most people are a little afraid. Most of us are women, but there are a few men. One man took some pictures to send to the IAWPC, but he made sure no one can see any faces, not even the reflection of a face so no one can be identified.'

'He also threw bottles with explosives in them to scare away the dogs before the authorities could arrive to kill them, but he was caught and investigated. They checked his phone and saw our chat groups, so I had to get a new number. But they can't charge him for what he did, because then they would have to admit they are killing dogs. And they are telling the whole world and FIFA that they are not doing this.'

'I'm afraid this man's experience has scared the rest of us though, the authorities are intimidating'.

'The Moroccans that don't support the killings also have to shut up because they want the World Cup, and other international events, here. There are a lot of investors coming here, building things like universities and new highways, and being the host for the World

Cup means more investors like that.

'Their livelihoods are at stake, if investors come there will be more money, more jobs, their children will have a better future'.

'But people that are allowed to abuse animals are dangerous. There was a recent example in Ben Hmad where they found several decapitated human bodies. The killer had done the same to dogs and cats first'.

'And once you open up your country to people from other places, tourists will come, and they all have phones and social media, and they can talk when they go home. You can't have a foot in both camps.'

Latifa has tried to get her daughter to talk to a psychologist, and although she agreed to go, she didn't open up about the animal cruelty issues.

'She is returning to her old self, but she is changed, she's focussing on schoolwork and we're trying to rebuild our relationship. I think she blames me in part, but reestablishing our relationship is what's most important to me.'

'She knows I'm working on behalf of the animals, and she's proud of that.'

'I won't stop, I want to get a large number of dogs adopted, I want to educate the next generation to be more caring towards animals, to change the mindset that dogs are unclean and shouldn't live in your house'.

'But I will have to continue to be careful about my identity, and make sure my face, or the face of my daughter, are never in the picture when I'm collecting evidence about the killings. I don't use my real name on social media either. I've also tried not to give any information out about myself when I've been asked and said that I'm not sure if I'm staying here or going back to the Netherlands'.

'There are thousands of people against the killings here in Morocco, but the government does a good job of silencing them'.

Hiding in Plain Sight

Hiding her identity from the authorities isn't something that **Juliet Gellatley** needs to do. She's the founder and director of Viva!, the leading UK vegan charity fighting for animal rights. Viva! was set up in 1994 and specialises in undercover investigations and high-profile animal campaigns. It focusses on factory farming, the environmental cost of animal agriculture and supports people on their journey into veganism. During its history Viva! has organised successful children's marches against live export, campaigned against religious slaughter, persuaded supermarkets to ban duck debeaking, recruited celebrities such as Joanna Lumley, Paul McCartney and Jerome Flynn to front campaigns, exposed conditions at the 'Happy Egg' farm and opposed the badger cull alongside its many groundbreaking undercover investigations.

But while Juliet doesn't have to hide who she is, what she believes and what she does, much of her work is still carried out in secret as she and her team work to expose the conditions animals are subject to in the name of food production and the conditions the industry would rather the public remained in the dark about.

'The secrecy I work with relates to being able to do the job of exposing what's happening to animals in factory farms, you're not exactly invited in with open arms to see the truth'.

'The primary reason we work undercover is because the conditions in which animals are kept in, the farmers know the public would find abhorrent'.

'We've developed a food system across the industrialised world, and beyond, which is cruel to animals, and there's no way around that. You're denying them all freedom, you're denying them everything that is natural to their life and to their being, and so to enable the public to feel comfortable with that, it's hidden behind closed doors'.

An example of Juliet's work is the multi-award-winning documentary *Hogwood*, available on Netflix. Following a tip off, Viva! sent a team of undercover investigators into Hogwood pig farm in Warwickshire. The team uncovered multiple instances of animal abuse and extreme welfare violations at the 'mega pig farm', which at the time was Red Tractor assured and supplying pork to Tesco. Red Tractor is a not-for-profit organisation founded in 2000 by the UK farming industry and food businesses to establish a single set of standards for UK food and drink. On its dedicated website, it says it 'champions high standards across the food chain, and our logo is the most recognised and most trusted farm assurance mark among UK consumers.' The network says its food chain assurance scheme includes over 42,000 UK farmers and over 600 food and drink processors and packers, and that it aims to deliver standards for British food that everyone can trust. All Red Tractor produce is traceable back to UK assured farms.

The Red Tractor scheme was in the news once again in August 2025 when footage obtained by *The Daily Mail* showed 'astonishing cruelty' and 'harrowing footage' at Somerby Top Farm in Lincolnshire.[3] *The Mail* reported that the farm has around 4,000 pigs, in sheds with up to 27 pigs per pen. It is a fattening farm run by Britain's largest pork supplier, where the animals are raised to reach the right weight for slaughter.

Juliet says, 'Our initial investigation at Hogwood showed clearly abhorrent things, like dead pigs left outside a shed on site. At that point I have to decide if it's worth escalating the investigation and what we're going to do with our findings.'

'With Hogwood I went in secretly first, then returned with colleagues. I decided we could not back off, that we had to find out who they were supplying and make a campaign because so many of the animals were in abject misery.'

'I walked into one of the sheds and there was an animal with ulceration, the skin was going black, deep into the bone. This hadn't happened overnight. Another pig was writhing in pain in front of me. These animals were being left to die in pain, not even being put out of their misery.'

'The footage was so bad that when we found out they were suppliers to Tesco, I thought I could let it be known I'd been inside the farm. I thought Tesco would withdraw, but it didn't, it dug its heels in and made excuses.'

'Instead, the farm spent £50,000 upping security, and I then had to decide if it was still safe to go back in. I can't physically fight people, probably very angry people, who don't want you there exposing what they don't want the public to see.'

Eventually, after a third Viva! investigation, Tesco dropped Hogwood Farm as a supplier and Red Tractor suspended the farm's certificate while an investigation took place.

'I do go into undercover investigations like this with a lot of trepidation, but I do it because the animals have no voice and I find what happens abhorrent.'

In the UK, over 1.2 billion land animals are slaughtered annually for food production,[4] this includes more than a billion chickens, millions of turkeys, pigs, sheep, and cattle.

'Viva! has been going for 31 years now, and when I first started investigating like this, I was one of the first people to do it. It was new ground, but I thought if I'm going to set up a vegan organisation, I needed to witness for myself what those animals are going through.'

'I don't pretend to be a massively brave person, I do find it scary, but I will continue to do it because the animals are still going through it, and factory farmers just want to become more intensive because of no other reason than economics.'

'So, I'm still going into factory farms and what I'm seeing is every bit as bad as what I was seeing 30 years ago.'

'I focus on the UK, and if we don't have undercover workers, we might have to go back into a place and put in hidden cameras. We might go in at night, when nobody can see but sometimes, we might have to film during the day and it's a risk.'

'If you are caught, they know why you're there, so being recognisable as being from Viva! makes no difference. We don't touch anything, we just film and get out.'

'Keeping the investigations secret isn't always an option though. When we visited the pig farm Flat House in Leicestershire, we decided to call the police and the RSPCA then and there because of the conditions. Another time we went to a farm and a cow was literally dying in front of us, so we abandoned our undercover work to immediately call a vet. And if you're calling people out at say 2am, then it's obvious what you were doing there.'

'With Hogwood when we filmed the appalling suffering of the animals, we thought we can't just leave and not tell the authorities, but other times we might wait to expose our findings so we can prepare the evidence and place it in the media.'

'At Flat House I went back the next morning after we'd been in and seen everything, I went to confront workers, to ask what they were going to do for these poor animals, by that point I'm not concealing who I am and what I've done, so I'm putting myself in danger, but farm animals have almost zero protection under law so I need to speak up.'

'We called the police and the RSPCA, they called the police too, so everything is out in the open then. Everything was handed over to Trading Standards and Flat House was prosecuted and was then shut down partly because the public had seen our evidence and what was going on.'

'So sometimes we do investigate in secret, but other times we waive our anonymity. Sometimes my face is on camera, so that I can explain the conditions to viewers and point out what's wrong. This is all decided on a case-by-case basis.'

'Of course, the industry itself is keeping the cruel conditions secret, an example of this is the gassing of pigs. Almost 90 per cent of pigs in the UK are killed by gassing. It causes agony as the carbon dioxide gas forms an acid on their eyes, nostrils, mouths and lungs.'

'And as well as the animal cruelty, factory farming and the impact of animal agriculture is one of the main causes of damage that's happening globally, it's just that people don't want to accept that.'

'One of the reasons that I do what I do, is because the industry itself has so much protection, I'm fighting a gigantic industry that is inherently cruel and damaging, and the government is complicit in that. I'm forced to work in secret.'

References

1. https://api.worldanimalprotection.org/country/morocco (accessed Sept 2025)
2. https://iawpc.org/morocco-dog-campaign/ (accessed Sept 2025)
3. https://www.dailymail.co.uk/news/article-15007039/Terrified-piglets-sickening-new-pork-farm-scandal.html (accessed Sept 2025)
4. https://committees.parliament.uk/writtenevidence/114481/html/#:~:text=This%20leaves%20UK%20farmers%20exposed,the%20dairy%20sector%20more%20widely. (accessed November 2025)

CHAPTER 3

Child Sexual Abuse and Domestic Abuse Campaigners

'Because I didn't know what abuse was, I didn't know I needed to tell someone, which is part of the work I do now, helping children identify when things should be queried, when trust has been broken.'

'From age nine to 44 I kept this secret' says Oxfordshire-based **Emma Jane Taylor**, a survivor of Child Sexual Abuse (CSA) and creator of the #NotMyShame campaign and movement.

'And when you're 52 and looking back at yourself, you think, why didn't I just say something? But there's a trauma bond between the abuser and the victim. He had become a family friend, and he had built up that trust.'

'You've got to be a certain type of person to think you can build that much trust that a child won't talk about what you've just done to them, a manipulator'.

Emma Jane's first experience of CSA was on a family holiday aged nine.

'The first incident was bizarre, I ran back inside, and I don't remember much else except that I didn't want to talk about it, I was terrified of speaking about it, and it was embarrassing.'

'At nine years old I was just happy hanging out with my parents, playing silly games with my brothers, building sandcastles. I was innocent and so there was no language and no awareness.'

'Because I didn't know what abuse was, I didn't know I needed to tell someone, which is part of the work I do now, helping children identify when things should be queried, when trust has been broken.'

In her charity work, Emma Jane now focusses on protecting children and having the difficult conversations that can prevent abuse from going unnoticed.

For Emma Jane the experience of CSA ran in parallel with something else she couldn't talk about. How her biological father, a man she perceived as 'handsome, funny and kind', told her when she was 11 that he wouldn't be seeing her anymore. Instead of picking her up every other weekend as normal, on the way back from her regular riding lesson he simply told his daughter that their relationship was over.

'I never talked about how horrible he was, because I thought he'd come back. I'd put him on a pedestal, and that became a pattern. I put bad people on pedestals and kept quiet out of shame.'

'Within a year I was sexually assaulted by a family friend who would go on to abuse me for nearly a decade.

'After my father left, I was heartbroken, I played Cliff Richard's 'Daddy's Home' on repeat and cried all the time. I was devastated and then the man turned up and became my friend.'

'I'd had so much taken from me at a young age that I was emotionally underdeveloped. This person came along and gave me presents, like jewellery and perfume, and money. But there was an expectation at the end of it. I knew no better.'

By age 13 this man, who was in his 40s, had taken Emma Jane's virginity, laughing when she bled during the rape.

'I was so scared, but I didn't go running home to tell my mum, I didn't tell my friends, and later he would tell me to do things, and I was like a robot, he gave me alcohol and drugs, and it took away the emotions.'

'I kept going back because this man gave me things that made me feel better, he told me to put pillows in my bed and leave the house in the middle of the night.'

'And I kept it all secret for nearly ten years because I had been manipulated to believe I liked this person.'

Her abuser was clearly practised at grooming, having found a way to manipulate Emma Jane into keeping quiet about what was happening.

'He made me feel like he cared about me, and having done things like sneak out of the house he'd made it so I would be in trouble too if I told on him.'

'It was coercive behaviour; I didn't tell people where I got the jacket, the jewellery, the perfume, the money from.'

'Eventually when I got to 16, I realised what was happening probably wasn't right. I'd flunked most of school, I tried to step away, but it took a long time.'

'I don't have a lot of memories from that time because I was traumatised, so you exist in a different state. It's a way for your mind to protect you, I can't remember conversations, I can't remember clothes.'

On the surface, Emma Jane had a settled family life, her mother had married her stepfather when she was around two years old. But her experiences with her two abusers and her father removing her from his life meant she held onto a lot of anger, that she didn't begin to process until she was a teenager. She stopped talking to her family and didn't communicate verbally with her mother for a year; she would get into the family car in silence. Now Emma Jane wonders why someone didn't ask what would make a young girl start to act like that, and what sort of trauma she might have experienced. Her silence was a warning sign that everyone ignored.

'Everyone assumed I behaved like I did because of what my father had done. It was great for my abuser; he could hide behind that. He was grooming the whole family and hidden in plain sight.'

'At school I was considered a juvenile delinquent, and they wanted to expel me. I had to be handed to the teachers each day and would sit in an office being watched while I did my schoolwork all day. Food was brought to me, and I was only allowed out to go to the bathroom. They put me in front of a psychiatrist but still no one got the cause of the problems.'

To cope, Emma Jane says she developed the ability to have multiple lives, depending on who she was with.

'I ended up as a party girl, drinking heavily, sniffing aerosols, taking drugs, off around the UK for a good time. But I'd come home and sob into my pillow because I was broken. Externally I looked happy, but I was broken, and there was only one way I was heading.'

'Eventually someone said to me you'll be dead or in prison by the time you're 20.'

This one statement was to set the wheels of her recovery in motion.

'Eventually I told a friend when I was 20, I wrote it all in a letter for her. Then I booked to see a therapist for 12 weeks. And the therapist encouraged me to tell my parents.'

'In the end I told my parents what had happened with the 'family friend' when I was about 23. They were heartbroken and felt awful. My stepfather asked me what I wanted to do about it, but I was too scared to do anything. So, I asked for their support while I continued going to therapy and set up my own business alongside treatment.'

'They were brilliant parents, but they were ill-equipped to deal with that level of trauma. That's not their fault, they come from a time when we didn't talk about this stuff, but they let me talk about it. When I wrote my book years later, they were worried that people would think they were bad parents, but they're not. They were groomed too, and by telling my story it will help others to see the blame lies only with the perpetrator.'

'I stayed in therapy off and on for the next 20 years, moving about to various therapies from acupuncture to reflexology, tapping to hypnotherapy, sound, water and picture therapies to psychotherapy, crystals to reiki. In the end my pets were probably the best therapy, and particularly my little Westie, Charlie.'

'When I got back in touch with old school friends, they also felt guilty they hadn't noticed what was going on, but there's only one person whose fault it is, and that's the perpetrator. They have all these memories of doing stuff together and photos of me, but I don't remember any of it because I had disassociated from it. And that time was taken from me alongside the physical abuse.'

'I fight so hard now because I had so much of my childhood taken. I was nine when it started and I was still coming out the other side of it when I was in my 40s.'

'But I had a supportive family, and during this time I also made some good memories. I set up my performing arts and my fitness businesses, I learnt Spanish, I became a hairdresser, I had a new lease of life.'

'But look at the devastation that the secrets I kept from friends and from my parents caused.'

But remaining silent is not Emma Jane's life today. She is a successful campaigner, an author, has regularly appeared on TV and radio discussing the topic of CSA, hosted events, spoken in Parliament, and in 2021 gave a TED talk entitled, "It's not just the strangers we should be careful of". She is the creator of the #NotMyShame campaign and movement and the founder of the Project 90-10 Charity; an educational programme designed for safeguarding leads to educate, campaign and raise awareness, and protect children from child sexual abuse.

'Would I be the woman I am today if I hadn't have gone through what I did? Maybe I would have healed and not been here as a campaigner. I have to pace myself alongside my professional career, but as a champion of this conversation I want to look back and know I don't have any more regrets that I have not spoken out.'

'It can take your breath away sometimes when you find yourself in the spotlight, or on the cover of a magazine, when I've been on stage presenting and talking about my story, with huge images of my face on a screen behind me. But then I remember my end goal is to give someone hope.'

'Sharing my story on a huge scale was liberating; afterwards I realised I do want to be here, while the majority of humans are good, there's a minority still hurting children. I've got braver and my fight has got stronger. While I never thought I'd start a campaign I'm now happy to share my story because I know I'm connecting to other people.'

'I get messages from people asking me not to stop, that it helps them, and that makes me realise why I campaign, why I run the charity.'

'If I can help one child, one adult, one survivor, one story, then that's better than nothing.'

So, what has Emma Jane learned about why victims of CSA often don't tell? For her it was because of the shame she felt and the manipulation by her abuser who used that.

'Keeping the secret was part of the abuse, the abuse wasn't just the rape, it was coercively separating me from other people with this secret, and using this secret as a weapon, so I couldn't reach out to the people that would help and support me.'

'Now I'm 52 and I look up and love the life I lead, the people I'm around. I have so much love for so many things. I've gone through that journey of removing that leech of shame and secrecy.'

'A couple of years ago I put out a message on social media that the abuse is not my shame. It went viral. So, I put it on a t-shirt. The campaign grew, it's bigger than me and everybody needs to engage with it.'

'We have town halls using it from Nottinghamshire to Wales, I have a team of volunteers and admin, we have a group of 600 people that have held onto shame and secrets, and people open up there because they've got support.'

Does Emma Jane have any regrets about telling the world about what happened to her?

'When I first shared my story, I thought is this going to be a car crash and affect my career? I was scared but I thought there must be so many people touched by this sort of thing. But I started speaking up and I'm thriving. People support the charity, they share messages, they donate and fundraise, people write and say, 'thank you' for speaking out.'

'I never had any expectations of getting to this point today, I just wanted to feel better.'

'It's my legacy, I don't have any regrets. Maybe when I go to my grave I'll have 'She had no shame' written on my head!'

I Don't Want to be His Secret

One in four women and one in six to seven men experience domestic abuse (DA).[1] This includes **Sam Beckinsale**, 58, best known for playing firefighter Kate Stevens in the hit TV show, *London's Burning*, who experienced living with a domestic abuser from her late 30s until her early 50s.

'We should be talking about Domestic Abuse, but only the people that are alive can do so, and only if they feel safe, and it's something they want to do. I don't think anybody who's experienced this should be ashamed for not speaking out.'

Sam was caught out due to believing the myth that DA meant physical violence only. But Sam's partner punished her on multiple levels every day for anything he considered wrongdoings, such as not cutting a slice of bread properly. He took her property, her money, isolated her from her family and friends, prevented her from working, and deprived her of sleep and healthy food and medical care. She found herself spending her days trying to please him, not knowing how she got into this situation with no means of escape as he controlled every aspect of her life, the psychological stress of which she describes as 'unbearable'.

'After I escaped, I realised I would never be the same. I went through a period where I didn't want to trust anyone, even myself, I didn't want to see or talk to anyone, even friends.'

'But once I was assured by professionals that his behaviour was nothing to do with me and that he would go on to do it again, I sat with that for a bit. I know absolutely someone's else behaviour is not my responsibility, but I felt complicit if I didn't say anything. I only intended to say it once and didn't expect years later to still be involved in the campaigning work I do today.'

'I just didn't want to be keeping his secrets; I still don't want to be his secret.'

'But you've got this constant battle going on inside yourself: do I stand up and say these things, and put my head above the parapet? And of course, the abuse still continues long after you've left.'

Sam understands however that it's not always possible to speak out, and that not everyone has some of the advantages she had.

'I chose to do it with the blessing of my family, and because I had a bit of a platform left [from being an actress]. I can use that now to help raise awareness for others.'

'But we run the risk of people being vilified if they don't speak out and vilified if they do.'

And speaking up can leave survivors of DA open to criticism and in danger.

'But the thing about being the lowest you can be is you've nothing left to lose. The only way is up. I'm not frightened of him anymore, I'm not frightened of being sued if I name him, I'm not frightened of his family or who he works for anymore. The threats no long work on me.'

Much of Sam's difficulty in speaking out came from a lack of language to name the type of abuse she suffered. The understanding of the concepts of psychological, emotional, economic abuse and controlling and coercive behaviour are relatively new, having only been formally criminalised ten years ago by the Serious Crime Act (2015).[2] Although this was part Sam's experience, like many others, she had no knowledge that what he was doing was illegal.'

In 2021, the Domestic Abuse Act changed the law by providing a statutory definition of domestic abuse, emphasising that domestic abuse is not limited to physical violence, but can also be emotional, controlling, coercive or economic. Post-separation coercive control and non-fatal strangulation were also recognised as criminal offences. It also banned the 'rough sex' defence, and clearly defined controlling someone's income or access to money as economic abuse. By defining individual offences within a domestic abuse case, each offense could be charged separately with its own legal definition and level of severity, allowing for a more proportional sentence.

'When the abuse started, there was no framework to discuss the abuse. Coercive control wasn't a thing; economic abuse wasn't a thing. Even today driving someone to death through abuse isn't illegal. They've tried to shoehorn it into manslaughter, but it's not accidental, it's deliberate. They know what they're doing.'

Now Sam likes to speak up about the uncomfortable truths about DA, and the things in our society that prevent other survivors from leaving and speaking out, and abusers being stopped.

In 2022, she wrote and helped create the docudrama *Love?* With Jason Figgis. It brought together the globally patterned lived experiences of many victims in order to raise awareness and depict coercive and controlling behaviour, so that it could be more clearly identified. An Internet Movie Database (IMDb.com) review described the film as 'a powerful film like no other'.

Sam points to fellow DA survivor Gisèle Pelicot, the 72-year-old French woman at the heart of the most extensive rape trial in French history, as someone who has eloquently captured one of the issues surrounding conversations about DA. When she faced the Vaucluse criminal court at her husband Dominique's rape trial in September 2024, Gisèle said simply, 'The shame isn't ours to feel, it's theirs'.

Gisèle was covertly drugged and raped by her husband Dominique and dozens of other men he invited to do so, over a nine-year period between 2011 and 2020. Dominique's crimes had only been discovered after he was arrested for upskirting, the practice of taking a photo or video under someone's clothes without their consent, at a supermarket in their hometown of Mazan, and his home computer was searched by police.

In October 2025, Gisèle told a French appeal court that she never gave consent for anyone to abuse her while she was in a comatose state and again said that no victim should ever feel shame. Husamettin Dogan, 44, a married father who was sentenced to nine years in prison during the original trial, had contested his conviction for rape. The court of appeal in Nîmes rejected his argument and extended his original nine-year jail term to 10 years.

Gisèle became a feminist icon, after waiving her right to anonymity as a sexual assault victim, to demand shame change sides. Following the case, there has been a call for changes in the French penal code on rape, which currently makes no clear mention of the need for a partner's consent. This means that to secure a guilty verdict in French courts, prosecutors must prove the intention to rape.

But Gisèle's impact extends far beyond her own country, as it has opened up a worldwide discussion on attitudes about and public understanding of sexual assault, including within marriage. Her stance on so publicly rejecting the so-called shame of being a survivor of rape has proved that speaking out about, and listening to, survivor accounts is of global importance. *Time* magazine named Gisèle as one of the most influential people of 2025.

Sam says, 'When someone dies, we understand it. We know the processes of grief and how people operate almost automatically up until the funeral, and after that the grief process begins. It can take years to heal, we accept that. We know when someone is burgled at home, it takes time for them to feel safe there again, they might even move. But we don't apply that same knowledge to victims of DA because it's still somehow seen as our fault, and that's where the shame comes in. But it's not our shame. We just don't blame victims of other crimes in the same way.'

'…it just adds to what the perpetrators have said that it's all our fault. When in reality, it's theirs.'

But Sam believes a lot of the silence and secrecy around DA isn't because the victims are keeping quiet to avoid shame and judgement, but rather that our political and legal system refuses to do anything about the issue.

'Women are forced to remain quiet through fear of retaliation, fear of judgement, fear of more humiliation, especially via our legal system, in criminal court cases,' says Sam.

Through Sam's work she often collaborates with Detective Superintendent Kristina Windsor, the domestic abuse lead at Avon and Somerset Police. Kristina believes her force sees 20 per cent of the people DA is affecting, meaning that 80 per cent of victims don't come forward.

'Less than a quarter of what's really going on is being reported. It's the UK's biggest crime and thus the police force's main business. It's the victim that has to bear the primary burden of DA, both the life cost and financially, and lives are taken week in, week out,' says Sam.

'And by Westminster ignoring the extent of this problem, it's like everybody is keeping the abusers' secrets.'

'I've been fighting to get so-called suicides of victims of domestic abuse recognised, they're not suicides in the normal sense, they are weaponised killings, murders.'

'This is a bigger problem than the dynamics of a so-called relationship between the survivor and the abuser. They've been told time and time again, research paper after research paper, data after data, 50 years of Women's Aid and we're still begging for help.'

'It's a financial decision in part, but if we faced up to this secret full on, we would have to do so much, change so many mechanisms.'

Woman's Aid is a national charity that grew out of the women's rights' movement in the 70s and 80s. It is now a federation of around 170 organisations that provide just under 300 local services to women and children across the country. It works to end domestic abuse against women and children via active campaigning and by providing frontline services.

The annual cost of domestic abuse in the UK is already estimated to be £85 billion.[3] This figure represents the combined impact of lost output, healthcare, criminal justice, and social care costs, as well as the profound personal costs to victims. But changing our approach would save money in the longer term.

'We're losing £85 billion a year, loss caused by the perpetrators and the system is haemorrhaging money. If you're in power, you could stop this.'

'And that's without considering longer-term costs, and the cost in terms of the children affected hasn't been looked at: their education, their health, that's not even in the data.'

Sam feels the political and legal systems are colluding with the perpetrators by not facing up to the problem head on.

'Modern marriage is an actual legal contract, born out of the feudal system, where you give up your identity, your possessions, your body even, with tax benefits, but entered into without legal advice currently as it's been given the gloss of being only about love. We've commercialised and politicised what is a personal love relationship. Our family courts operate in secret with absolutely no accountability to anybody outside of them; somebody going into a family court as a victim of abuse is legally not allowed to tell other family members what is going on in there.'

'A minimum of one in 20 adults in England and Wales is a perpetrator of domestic violence. One Sunday afternoon with Carrie Bower of Hourglass, we worked out that meant 27 Wembley stadiums full of perpetrators, but we've only got one Wembley stadium full of prison places for ALL criminals.'

Hourglass is a charity dedicated to ending the harm, abuse and exploitation of older people in the UK, and runs free-to-call 24/7 helpline. Around 2.6 million people over the age of 65 are victims of abuse each year in the UK, which includes domestic abuse alongside, physical, psychological, economic and sexual abuse and neglect.

The sums are a response to the National Policing Statement on Violence Against Women and Girls (VAWG) published a year ago,[4] where the College of Policing and the National Police Chiefs Council (NPCC) identified 20 per cent of all recorded crime in England and Wales in 2022-23 as VAWG-related. It said that at least one in 12 women will be a victim of VAWG every year, with one in 20 adults in England and Wales being a perpetrator of VAWG each year.

'As a society, we're keeping this quiet, it's a secret from the public, but if you look at the figures it's all there.'

'Every domestic homicide review investigation costs something like £3 million, that's a terrific amount of dissonance going on.'

Sam believes that while an abuser ensures you don't have the mental space to think of the steps you can take to escape, and erodes your social support network, those that do speak up find that there's nothing beyond the abusive relationship to help them feel safe.

'There's a big push to get people to report DA but there's no safety planning, no belief and no accountability. They're told to leave an abuser, but we know that's the most dangerous time for them, their loved ones and their animals, and for the next 18 months.'

'There's nothing there for them, the system is endangering them by not being fit for purpose and it's based on the feudalism of the marriage contract.'

'In terms of safety for your children after you've left, the law says that parental responsibility rights are automatically afforded no matter what a parent does. If you've got a safe and an unsafe parent, the safe parent is trying to keep the child safe, doing what they are legally bound to do, protect the child, safeguard the child, but if they keep the child away from the unsafe parent, they could go to prison for it.'

'Perpetrators have different brains,[5] you can see this on scans, and it would be great to be able to use that evidentially. The damage done to children's and young people's brains before they are fully formed is proven, it's there, it's a physical thing from emotional, psychological harm.[6] Abuse causes brain damage for the rest of their lives unless they get the support they need. We need that put in place for those leaving abuse.'

'Even with a fully-formed adult brain, when we are in a dangerous place our brain does not allow us to think in the same way as it does when we are safe. Survival is its only priority and that can impact our decisions, which may not appear logical to others. But it is to us.'

'The biggest thing we need to do is get those people safe, and we need to be protected while we sort out our lives.'

'There's a view that people who have been abused are weak and pathetic, but they have been forced to develop so many skills, they're the best risk assessors that exist.'

Sam would also like to see employers taking responsibility alongside our legal system stepping up.

'Our business community could be doing a lot; it should be statutory for every organisation and business to have a DA policy. We could raise sentencing on coercive control too, in line with Australia, which has the same legal system as us.'

'Our coercive and controlling behaviour law is 10 years old, it's not new, and yet there's still hardly any prosecutions, so clearly we can't police our way out of it.'

'But unless we talk about it, we're not tackling the culture, we're not tackling the systemic elements.'

Sam points out that police forces across the country aren't trained on DA in a consistent way and that you have to report the crime to your local force, regardless of their experience in policing that crime.

'You also have to train the Crown Prosecution Service (CPS)in these cases. If you get to court you have to train judges, but it's the jury that decides guilt, and that's why we need to talk about it with the public. Unless we talk about it, and in the same way we talk about any other crime, we can't rely on the criminal justice route.'

And not talking about DA might particularly affect our younger generations, with a recent report stating that in the UK, young people aged 16 to 20 experience domestic abuse at higher rates than older age groups.[7] Specifically, 8.7% of those aged 16 to 19 and 7.1% of those aged 20 to 24 reported experiencing some domestic abuse in the year ending March 2024. This is higher than in older age groups, such as those aged 55 and over. The report showed that approximately one in five (20.5%) people aged 16 and over have experienced domestic abuse since the age of 16.

It's good news then that Sam recently spoke to Strode College students when the Avon and Somerset Police held a community DA conference with input from young students themselves. Teenagers face challenges unique to their generation and keeping communication open so that anyone experiencing abuse can speak up is essential.

'Our young people are growing up expecting to be abused. Anyone born after 2005 has had the internet at the heart of their relationships. They've had porn thrust in their faces, and a tech industry that is doing nothing to ensure you opt out of that. But their parents, born before this, are telling them how to have relationships that they have no experience of.'

'They've also been through a pandemic, and they are isolated. Social skills are difficult for them; they always have their heads in their phones. Drama has been cut from our schools so they can't safely explore feelings, emotions and scenarios, and there's no way to begin to explore conversations.'

But this is not a problem just for the future generations to deal with.

Domestic abuse victim studies show a correlation between domestic violence and poorer health outcomes. Victims of domestic violence are at higher risk for certain cancers, like cervical cancer, and autoimmune diseases like lupus. They also face increased risks of chronic conditions, mental health issues, and lower overall quality of life, which can indirectly affect life expectancy.[8]

'The idea that psychological and emotional abuse isn't causing physical harm is wrong. It impacts the brain, it impacts the nervous and the immune system,' says Sam.

'We have to stop ignoring what goes on behind closed doors, thinking that an Englishman's home is his castle, fearing the nanny state. We are in the 21st century but we're living with systems based on society which existed hundreds of years ago.

'We look at other countries and say they're subjugating women, but it wasn't until my 20s that it wasn't illegal for my husband to rape me and even today, you've got a different tariff when a man kills a woman in the home to when a man kills a woman on the street, by 10 years. That's 10 years less for murdering her in her home. That is state-sanctioned.'

'We don't need new laws, we've got plenty – Actual Bodily Harm (ABH), Grievous Bodily Harm (GBH) – we just need to make them equitable and ensure there is the political will to use them and impose accountability and restrictions on criminal domestic abusers, instead of their victims, even if we don't have the prison spaces. It's about there being the systemic will to actually change things.'

'We need a revolutionary response to DA. We've seen change occur with attitudes to drink driving; we've done it with smoking. We can all help by talking about it and getting the information I didn't have out there.'

References

1. https://www.ons.gov.uk/peoplepopulationandcommunity/crimeandjustice/bulletins/domesticabuseinenglandandwalesoverview/november2024 (accessed Sept 2025)

2. https://www.legislation.gov.uk/ukpga/2015/9/section/76 (accessed Nov 2025)

3. https://domesticabusecommissioner.uk/wp-content/uploads/2025/06/dac_bcyp_main_report_V6-DIGITAL.pdf (accessed Sept 2025)

4. https://cdn.prgloo.com/media/034ed60aa6564c1fbdcfb03fd8e6a210.pdf (accessed Sept 2025)

5. https://pmc.ncbi.nlm.nih.gov/articles/PMC4847704/ (accessed Sept 2025)

6. https://www.bath.ac.uk/announcements/brain-differences-seen-in-children-with-conduct-disorder-depend-on-abuse-history/ (accessed Sept 2025)

7. https://www.ons.gov.uk/peoplepopulationandcommunity/crimeandjustice/articles/domesticabusevictimcharacteristicsenglandandwales/yearendingmarch2024 (accessed Sept 2025)

8. https://pubmed.ncbi.nlm.nih.gov/27943059/, https://pmc.ncbi.nlm.nih.gov/articles/PMC11339029/, https://www.cih.org/media/nwkbvk5h/0305-domestic-abuse-campaign-the-pledge-nov2024.pdf (accessed Sept 2025)

CHAPTER 4

The Sexual Assault Survivor

'One time he came into my room and wanted to do stuff, I didn't want to do stuff, but he pushed on and did it anyway and I kind of froze. I didn't know how to react.'

Ella was 15 when the Covid lockdown happened in 2020 and at the time another family had come to live in her home as part of a 'bubble'. This included the son of the family, who was two years older than Ella.

'I'd always had a crush on this boy and was happy when I found out that my feelings were reciprocated. We ended up sneaking around the house to kiss and stuff. I thought it was thrilling and grown up.'

But Ella soon found herself in a difficult position.

'He always wanted to take things further than I was comfortable with, and I felt immense guilt because my father is very involved in the church and I was brought up not to do stuff like this, and to keep myself untouched because otherwise I would be worthless. I felt guilt for being with him, and guilt for being in a secret relationship, particularly as his twin sister and my brother and sister were also around, and we hadn't told them.'

'One time he came into my room and wanted to do stuff, I didn't want to do stuff, but he pushed on and did it anyway and I kind of froze. I didn't know how to react.'

After the event, the boy apologised to Ella, claiming he hadn't meant to do what he had done, that he felt bad, and that he didn't want Ella to think badly of him for it.

'I told myself that it was okay, that he hadn't raped me, and that he'd just kind of pushed me, that he did what he wanted and left. I didn't think it constituted sexual assault. I thought maybe it was fine because we were in a relationship and that just happens.'

'But immediately after he went back to threatening me, saying that if I didn't give him what he wanted it would be very easy for him to come and rape me, and that he'd been in my room while I was asleep and I hadn't even known. It was scary.'

Thankfully the visiting family moved on from Ella's home, and she hasn't spoken to or seen anyone from the family since.

'I don't think his family knew what happened, but I think they suspected that we had feelings for each other before everything happened.'

Ella was left feeling confused by and guilty about what had happened, and decided against reporting the assault, partly because she did not recognise what it was at the time. She was perhaps too young and inexperienced to fully understand how the perpetrator had manipulated her.

'I didn't report it to anyone because I didn't think it constituted an assault at the time, and I also didn't want my parents to know what had happened, that I'd been in a relationship with him and that I'd been sneaking around. I didn't see the point. I didn't think I was going to get any justice.'

Ella felt very alone dealing with her feelings after the assault and coped as best she could.

'I forced myself not to think about it and repressed it, and because I knew it was something I couldn't talk about as freely as I would want to, or go to anyone for any kind of help, I would make myself not think about it. At times it would come back, and I'd feel confused, and ask why is this appearing? Why am I struggling with this? Why am I feeling like this? But as the years have gone on… it's five years ago, I do feel a bit more comfortable. I can speak about it now, but it was tough initially, especially for the first couple of months.'

It's taken Ella, who is now at university, several years to process what has happened. Time that would typically make bringing criminal proceedings far more difficult.

During this time, she learnt about the not-for-profit organisation Enough, which distributes self-testing kits that allow those who suspect they have been sexually assaulted to take a home swab and get it tested for DNA, and have the results stored. Storing the results can give the victim the much-needed time to heal and decide how they want to proceed. The kits also validate that there has been a physical assault, removing any doubt that contact has happened.

Because of her experience, Ella became an ambassador for Enough.

'A few years later I told some friends, people that I trusted, and when I started working with Enough, I told them.'

'Since then I've told my mum, but not in full, but I've not told my dad.'

Once Ella was able to talk about her experience, she was also able to better understand what had happened to her.

'Talking about it with others has helped me acknowledge what happened was actually sexual assault, even though I told myself at the time that it wasn't. Because we were in a relationship, I thought it must have been fine, but I realise that it's not okay.'

The feminist charity Rape Crisis, which has its origins in the 1970s and 1980s, says that one in four women have been raped or sexually assaulted since the age of 16. It also says 71,227 rapes were recorded by police in 2024 but that by the end of 2024, charges had been brought in just 2.7% of these cases. This means that fewer than three in one hundred rapes recorded by police in 2024 resulted in someone being charged that same year let alone convicted.[1]

Rape Crisis is the membership organisation for 36 Rape Crisis centres across England and Wales. It delivers specialist services to those affected by sexual violence and abuse, and aims to educate, influence and make change. It sets out to achieve its goal by believing victims and survivors, by helping them to get their voices heard and by fighting for victims and survivors to have access to specialist support. It also raises awareness about the prevalence and impacts of sexual violence and abuse, challenges rape culture, and works to influence change in public policy relating to sexual violence and abuse.

Now Ella hands out the Enough self-test kits at universities, creates social media content, talks to people to let them know more about the charity and the social events it runs in cafes, bars and restaurants around Bristol.

'A lot of people who support Enough and a lot of people that take the kits say they wish these kits had been around when they suffered a similar experience to mine. It's upsetting to hear that so many people have had this sort of thing happen, but it shows the kits can make a difference.'

Using an Enough kit takes five minutes. Half of the sample is frozen, which means it can be passed on to the police later if the owner of the sample wants that. Then the United Kingdom Accreditation Service (UKAS)-accredited lab uses the other half for the test, keeping it on record unless asked to destroy it. The results are available online after one day, and users are notified that the results are available by email.

'Discussing the variety of things that other people have experienced with them makes me feel supported; a big issue with me was that I didn't think my assault was serious enough, that it didn't necessarily matter. But hearing stories from different people has made me realise that sexual assault isn't a one-size-fits-all thing. There's no stereotype that fits what counts as an assault. It can happen in different ways, and in every single way it does happen, it counts.'

Working through her ordeal has given Ella more of an understanding as to why she found defining what happened to her as an assault.

'I think the culture around discussing assault and consent is improving but there's a long way to go. We still find when we're handing out Enough kits that people say, 'I don't want to talk about that' or some men say, 'I don't think I need a kit, that's not something that can happen to me,' so there's still a lot of stigma attached to speaking up about your own experiences and the repercussions seem to affect the survivor rather than the perpetrator. It's still a very big problem, but compared to when my parents were younger, there's definitely more discussion and more awareness.'

Rape Crisis figures show that one in two rapes against women are carried out by their partner or ex-partner and that six in seven rapes against women are carried out by someone they know.[2]

Ella would like to see change, including people speaking up on behalf of victims.

'In the future I'd like to see more open conversation and less of an emphasis on the survivor being shamed, and more shame on the perpetrator because it's solely on the perpetrator.'

'I think we also need more of an understanding that the current justice system may not work for everybody, because everybody's experience may not be the same. As someone who never even considered the police, and that had an experience some might think does not fit into a conventional definition of assault, I think the Enough kits are useful. If I had access to a kit at that time, even if I didn't decide to proceed with any criminal charges, it definitely would have helped me to know what had happened was an assault and that it is still valid, even if other people don't see it like that.'

In fact, most survivors don't report it to the police, Rape Crisis research shows that five in six women who are raped don't report it, but that many of these survivors do tell someone else what happened. The reasons survivors don't tell the police were embarrassment (40 per cent); they didn't think the police could help (38 per cent); and humiliation (34 per cent).[3]

As well as the definition of assault being a problem, Ella is also aware that stigma played a part in her not speaking up at the time of her assault, and that there's a judgement upon women who haven't 'kept themselves safe' even though it's not their responsibility to do so.

'I think there's always been so much in society with women's bodies being policed and that expectation that if you go out at night you need to have this and that, you need your keys, you need to be on your phone [talking to someone for safety], you need to be dressed in a certain way and not put yourself in dangerous situations. It's always been societal to put this expectation on women. But it's not a fair argument, because despite all this, assault and rape still happen. It's not something you can prevent or fight against. But there's always been a policing of women to make sure we're protecting ourselves and keeping safe, when reality shows us it's not something that we can always do.'

The result of the recent trial that American singer Cassie Ventura brought against American rapper and record producer Sean 'Diddy' Combs shows just how hard it is to protect a survivor and convict an abuser. Commentators have suggested that the failure of the jury to convict Combs of racketeering and sex trafficking charges, instead convicting him on two lesser counts of transportation to engage in prostitution will deter survivors from coming forward. Cassie's testimony was supported by numerous photos, videos and witness testimonies, but she was still subjected to victim blaming that asked why she didn't leave sooner and calling her complicit in what happened, while the defence, instead of denying violence by Combs, claimed it was mutual.

In Ella's case, her culture and upbringing also reinforced a need to keep quiet.

'The church played a massive role in how I thought I should behave as a woman. I was petrified because I'd always heard talk of once a woman has sex before marriage, or if she does anything with a man before marriage, then she's not pure and she's not whole anymore. And that if anything happens to me like that then my life is ruined. A lot of culture is intertwined with these beliefs. I come from a culture that is also quite misogynistic and places a lot of emphasis on women being at fault and women having to keep themselves pure. I think then that bleeds into religion, which interprets it any way it wishes.'

In the future if Ella were to have children, she'd tackle these difficult conversations early on.

'I would want any children I had to be treated equally, whatever their gender. I would never want my daughter to grow up feeling like she's inferior or like every sort of blame belongs to her, or that she can't do anything a son could do.'

'And I would definitely have conversations about consent and self-confidence earlier. In my case, at the time of my assault, my self-esteem was quite low. I think if self-confidence had been instilled in me and I'd had that kind of conversation I wouldn't have felt the need to have been sneaking around with this boy who was older than me and doing things I didn't want to do. But I felt that I had to because this is how it is, this is how love is. Obviously, it wasn't love. Consent would definitely be something I would speak to my children about and instilling self-confidence.'

Ella is now studying for a career in social justice and welfare, through which she can support and help people.

'I think my experience has shaped my choices for the future, just wanting to make sure that people who don't necessarily feel powerful know that they can speak up.'

References

1. https://rapecrisis.org.uk/get-informed/statistics-sexual-violence/ (accessed Sept 2025)

2. https://rapecrisis.org.uk/get-informed/statistics-sexual-violence/ (accessed Sept 2025)

3. https://rapecrisis.org.uk/get-informed/statistics-sexual-violence/ (accessed Sept 2025)

SECTION 2

WORK AND SELF-DEVELOPMENT

CHAPTER 5

Wartime Bombe Operator

'She must have come home on leave, and I don't know what my mother thought her daughter was doing, so either Barbara came up with some tall tales or my mother knew better than to ask.'

The Government Code and Cypher School (GC&CS) at Bletchley Park in Buckinghamshire was the top-secret home to the World War II 'Ultra' intelligence project, famed for cracking enemy messages encrypted using the German Enigma and Tunny cipher machines. The Enigma Code was considered one of the most effective encryption devices ever invented because of its complicated electromechanical design and frequent key changes. Alan Turing and Gordon Welchman at the GC&CS designed equipment to help the code-cracking work carried out at Bletchley, including the bulky electromechanical code-breaking machines called 'Bombes'.

Until 1942, Bletchley Park also received and transmitted initial messages from the Special Operations Executive (SOE) that Churchill had set up two years earlier to enable espionage, sabotage and subversion in enemy-occupied Europe.

By 1945 Bletchley was employing almost 9,000 people, 75 per cent of whom were women and almost everyone who worked for Bletchley Park signed the Official Secrets Act (OSA), with no expiry date to their contract. This meant no discussing what you were up to on a day-to-day basis, even in precious letters home. Staff remained bound by the OSA even when the war ended and were warned that they would be unable to talk about their activity at Bletchley for many years. Penalties for breaking the OSA were harsh, including fines and imprisonment. In 1940 The Treachery Act was passed to cover acts of betrayal against the UK and carried the death penalty. There's little doubt the personnel took this seriously.

Talking about Bletchley after the war Churchill said the people who worked there were 'the geese that laid the golden egg but never cackled.' It's believed that the code-breaking efforts at Bletchley Park significantly shortened World War II by at least two years, and perhaps even four.[1]

The revelations about Bletchley's role in the war only came to the public's attention in 1974 when a former member of the British secret service, Frederick Willam Winterbotham, published his memoir *The Ultra Secret*. During the war Winterbotham had overseen distributing the intelligence data gathered at Bletchley to Winston Churchill and British field commands around the world. Several subsequent memoirs have proved that in wartime breaking the enemy codes is as important as it gets, although much of history has failed to highlight the role of women in delivering the victory.

From 1942 onwards, the Women's Royal Naval Service (WRNS or 'Wrens') became the sole operators of the Bombe machines. Eastcote was the largest code-breaking Bombe outstation of Bletchley and came into operation in September 1943. Converted from government buildings in Hillingdon, north-west London, it was home to up to 100 Bombes of different types, Wren Bombe operators, Royal Air Force (RAF) mechanics, and associated staff. By the summer of 1944, there were 1,676 Wrens tending 211 Bombe machines, mainly in outstations like Eastcote and Stanmore. At its peak there were 824 female Bombe operators at Eastcote compared to 142 male RAF mechanics.

One of those Wrens was Barbara Mary Allen (née Grigg) who joined up in 1942 when she was just 17.

Her sister Jo Cunningham, now in her eighties and living in a village in Berkshire, was just three years old when her sister headed off to join the war effort. Their father was serving in the Royal Engineers, and their mother had taken in evacuees from London. To make space for these house guests, each night oldest daughter Barbara was sent to sleep at her grandparents' house, on the other side of town.

'Barbara was glad to join the Wrens, and get away, she wanted something different,' says Jo.

'As adults, my other sister was a secretary to a film agent, while I travelled a lot because my husband was in the Air Force, and I always thought we had the more interesting lives, but much later I discovered Barbara had had this secret life as a Bombe operator at Eastcote during the war, and I didn't know anything about it until she was well into her eighties!'

'I know that she was given the job at Eastcote after being called into the office there and told that she'd been selected for a mission because she was well educated. They told her very little, just said that it was important. She didn't know what she was going to be doing but didn't want to say no.'

'She said it was quite boring, the machine clicked over and over again, and if it stopped then they'd realise they had something and send it over to Bletchley.'

The Bombe machines were described by operators as having the appearance of big metal bookshelves, housed along a huge corridor with wings of the main building named after countries the Germans had occupied. The outstation had armed guards, and the blocks were covered in barbed wire. The Wrens worked in shifts, 24 hours a day and performed military drills, sleeping in dormitories when they weren't working. Everyone was expected to work to a high standard despite the work itself being quite monotonous.

When the Bombes were dismantled after the war, those who had worked on them were allowed to take a piece, such as a switch, as a souvenir.

'When she left Eastcote, they needed drivers, so even though she couldn't drive she put her name down, and she stayed as a driver for the rest of the war.'

'We only found out about Barbara's role in the war because a man researching Bletchley somehow tracked her down and came to talk to her about it all. She took part in oral history recordings, and that's held in their exhibition now, which is lovely to hear if you visit.'

It's true to say that attitudes to sharing information about the war have changed, and the feeling now is that everything about World War II should be documented and explained, particularly now that fewer veterans remain alive to tell us their experience first-hand.

'Despite the big age gap, I was very close to both my older sisters, Barbara and Pat, who were just two years apart in age. In fact, I felt like I had three mothers growing up!'

'When I went to Bletchley myself, and when I watch the films that have highlighted a lot of what went on there, I thought, she did all this and I never knew about it; there were all these ladies her sort of age there doing this, and none of them blabbed.'

'When she was older, Barbara went to work on the railway, in the accounts office and she met her future husband at one of the dances held there. She got married and had four children. She moved back to live around the corner from our mother, so she was born and died in the same street, and I'm sure most of her neighbours never had any idea of the part she'd played in the war.'

'In terms of friends she made there, she mentioned a few names, but she never saw them again after Bletchley.'

In fact, the majority of the women who served in the war returned to their old lives when it ended; they married, had children and got on with their lives. They'd signed the OSA and remained guarded for the rest of their lives. It's likely that until the files were declassified, they were reluctant to meet up with ex-colleagues to discuss old times. Even at the time, since there was no work chit-chat allowed, it was hard for those in one department to see the bigger picture, so they often didn't know the real importance of the work they were doing.

'When she was at Eastcote, Barbara and the other Wrens used to go up to London together a lot, she said that once they were all in Trafalgar Square watching the doodlebugs passing over, and a man came up and told them off for not taking cover.'

'They also used to get tickets to all the theatres, she said they saw some wonderful shows and watched Laurence Olivier on stage.'

'She must have come home on leave, and I don't know what my mother thought her daughter was doing, so either Barbara came up with some tall tales or my mother knew better than to ask.'

At the time, the Ministry of Information (MOI), a government department established at the start of the war, often ran campaigns designed to discourage 'careless talk' between service personnel, friends and family, as well as the general public – suggesting that enemy spies could be listening in. While Barbara and her colleagues would have been reminded by their superiors not to give away any minor detail about their work, including in letters home, her mother would have been familiar with MOI slogans like 'Loose Talk Can Cost Lives'.

'My husband and I did go to a veterans' event at Bletchley with Barbara and one of her daughters. She was in her early 90s by then, and she had a little badge on to show who she was.'

'When we visited, Barbara showed us the hut she worked in, and where the messages would have gone.'

'I think there are several reasons Barbara didn't talk about her time at Bletchley for years after; one was that my father didn't talk about his wartime experiences. He was on a ship coming back from Palestine when it got torpedoed. He was rescued from the water, but he never spoke about it. He had some terrible times, and I think he didn't want to relive them, so she might have thought she should also remain quiet about her war years.'

'Possibly she might have thought of it as boasting. You don't go to a cocktail party and tell people what you used to do, you sort of gloss over that and talk about what you're doing now.'

'It's such a shame because so many women helped in the war effort, carrying on at home, doing munitions, building aircraft and helping here and there, working quietly in the background. They really are unsung heroes.'

'Barbara told the chap who came to interview her about Bletchley that she didn't talk about her time there because she didn't want people to know how old it would make her! Our mother was the same, never wanting to admit her age.'

'Us Brits can be a cold lot too. If you look at the Italians, the Spanish and the French, they're so open, and we're so reserved.'

The GC&CS left Bletchley Park in 1946 to move to Eastcote, and later Cheltenham, where it is based today, now known as Government Communications Headquarters (GCHQ). In 1993 Bletchley Park opened as a museum dedicated to showcasing the achievements of Britain's World War II code-breakers. However, the legacy and expertise of many of the women involved in the process has often been overlooked.

While the Wrens like Barbara were not code-breakers, and knew nothing of cryptanalysis, the Bombe operators at Eastcote and Bletchley's other outstations were essential. Without the personnel to operate the machines and keep the outstations running, the entire Enigma code-cracking process wouldn't have been able to operate so effectively.

Like Barbara, it seems many of the former Bombe operators were humble about the part they played in the war via their time at Eastcote. Typically, they were there for a few years and they were young, and life just carried on after the war in the way it did for many. Since many people were called up and helped with the war effort one way or another, their role may not have seemed any more important than anyone else's to them. And of course, part of their training was to accept that they were a small part in a bigger organisation.

Listed on the Roll of Honour, Barbara died in 2021 but will live on through the memories of her, and the role she and fellow Wrens played in shortening the war through helping with the code-breaking process, all now held at Bletchley.

'I wish I had spoken to her a lot more about it,' says Jo, 'but I'm pleased she'll be remembered for it now.'

References
1. https://www.britishlegion.org.uk/get-involved/remembrance/stories/alan-turing-legacy (accessed Sept 2025)

CHAPTER 6

Private Investigators and Mystery Shopping

'Some of the undercover jobs can be scary; the people you are investigating, are by the nature of the investigation, not that nice.'

Jen Jarvie, 50, used to visit up to 100 shops within a fortnight when she was employed as a professional mystery shopper, covering a huge area in the Northeast of England. She worked for large chains, including the Card Factory and Waterstones, plus garages and supermarkets such as Sainsbury's, checking that shops and employees were delivering the prescribed brand experience.

The job appealed to Jen as she knew she'd be able to fit her work around her family.

One of the easiest ways she blended in was by taking her pre-school-aged daughter with her as her cover.

'Everyone just assumed I wouldn't be working if I had my daughter with me. We'd mystery shop in Clarks for example. At one time she had more shoes than anyone I have ever met!'

'I'd end up with my car boot full of food, and even the back seats, I'd have to stop for the day and drop donations off at the Salvation Army.'

'It was the ultimate undercover job that you were paid for. My daughter would often ask to skip nursery and come with me to the shops; she's so sociable now because of that, I think! One day we'd be in Leeds, the next Newcastle, another day it would be Hull.'

But it wasn't just a case of enjoying a shopping spree, and getting paid for it. Her work required specific skills.

'When I went into the retailers I'd have to memorise five different interactions, with specific questions and memorise the answers, then once I'd left, I had to fill in paperwork noting everything down verbatim, and describe how they'd looked, their mannerisms.'

'I'd also be paid to go into somewhere like Asda and deliberately drop a bottle of wine, to check how responsive the staff were, how quickly it was cleaned up.'

'I've even sat tests and deliberately cheated, perhaps using an obvious calculator, when that is not allowed, so that the companies running them can see if the test is being invigilated properly. In this instance, I wasn't trying to blend in but actually trying to get noticed and get myself thrown out!'

Mostly though, Jen had to learn how to blend into the background.

'When I was a mystery shopper I deliberately dressed in a mundane way, nothing that anyone would be able to remember. It's the opposite of how I've since learnt to promote my own business. Now I'd never go to a networking meeting if I wasn't wearing something bright!'

After mystery shoppers were easily and cheaply replaced by digital feedback options, Jen decided to study Death Investigation at Teesside University, and graduated with a first-class honours degree. A back injury following a car accident meant she was unable to go into the police force, so instead she taught professional policing, until she began her career as a full-time private investigator. Now she combines her work with studying for a PhD. She is currently working on a comparative study between the methods that police use for cold cases versus those used by armchair detectives; amateur enthusiasts typically not directly involved in the case, working from home under their own steam often using second hand information and online forums.

'I've now worked as a private investigator for 13 years, predominantly looking at historical murders, and predominantly working for the family or friends of the deceased who feel the police investigation hasn't gone far enough.'

'I've also been contacted by Facebook groups before; they are sort of armchair detectives.'

Typically, the cases Jen takes on are 20 to 30 years old.

'At the time those who knew the deceased will have had faith in the police, but over time, if nothing's been discovered, the belief has waned. They want a fresh pair of eyes, and often it's out of desperation.'

When taking a job, Jen has to consider her personal safety.

'Some of the undercover jobs can be scary; the people you are investigating, are by the nature of the investigation, not that nice.'

'I also have to make a judgment call if I'm contacted by someone who says they have some evidence they want me to look at and they want to meet; I have to weigh that up and consider safety.'

'I've prepped clients to be ready to run for it on my say-so, and taken boxing classes myself to ensure undercover work is slightly less scary.'

'On the flip side of this, the client's also put a lot of trust in me. Many have never used a private investigator before, and don't know anyone else that has either. They've got to trust me with the worst thing that's ever happened to them.'

'The industry isn't regulated in the UK, but I'm part of the Association of British Investigators; we're vetted and scrutinised annually. There's a voluntary code of conduct, and you are interviewed by a panel before you can join. There's a yearly membership fee too.'

While Jen follows an ethical code laid out by her professional body, the trust must work both ways.

'I have to trust the client too, and it's not always a family.'

'If I find something out, the client might want to go public with it, to push the case towards being solved. They can be quite desperate for a breakthrough. But it's not always a good idea, and we have to discuss that, as the wrong move could jeopardise a case.'

'Before I take a case, I have to have certain difficult conversations, I have to know if I might discover that they are responsible for a crime. There must be complete honesty between me and the client. And they must understand that if that honesty is broken, I have a moral duty and won't hesitate to go to the police.'

'In a way, my real client is the person that has died, the living people I speak to are just their advocates.'

Being a private investigator allows Jen to work undercover and gain access to places and information hidden to others.

'I absolutely love my job, and that includes the secretive nature of it.'

'I enjoy the variety it brings, but also the feeling that I often know more than the general public about a case. I've got the privilege of having access to information that only a few people have.'

'I am limited in what I can tell people about my job. Friends might ask, or if I tell someone what I do for a living, they inevitably ask more, and often about my views on well-known cases like the disappearance of Madeleine McCann, or something that's currently in the news.'

'But I'm dealing with things that are pretty horrific, like child murder and I tend to deal with a lot more cases of femicide than anything else. People want the gossip, but I have to be careful, even for self-preservation.'

Being a woman might give Jen a professional edge in the secret world of private investigation.

'As a female private investigator, I think I'm more apt to empathise with the family. Officials like the police might be more matter of fact or colder because of their training, even the female officers.'

'But that said, whether it's because I'm a woman or because I'm a private investigator *and* a woman, when I've spoken to families, they've said that I've stopped and listened, that they've felt heard.

But with the police sometimes they have felt like they're shouting and no one's listening. And a lot of the cold-case work is carried out by male police officers. Is it because I'm female or is it because they are my client, and I'm more accountable to them?'

'I have been in police headquarters before and everyone else in the room was male, and someone said, 'Could the little girl leave the room please?', I looked around expecting to see a child, but they were talking about me, and I was 44 at the time!'

'I have people come to me not wanting to talk to the police; they see them as problematic. But I still have to make sure that ethically and morally I'm on the right side of the fence.'

'I think everybody lies and everybody keeps secrets, whether they are big or small lies, from planning surprise parties to real mind-blowing information. But there can be a dark side to it in my work, things a client has told you that you can't reveal, and I have to carry that secret'.

Protecting Yourself and Your Client

'Most of my work is covert,' says **Sarah Martin**, who is in her 50s and runs her own investigation agency. 'And I'm aware that people I approach can be quite intimidated, whether I'm tracing witnesses or undertaking door-to-door enquiries, but being female can put people at ease, particularly if the person I'm approaching is a female, who may otherwise feel physically vulnerable when a stranger approaches.'

'If I'm on surveillance in a car, say, it's easy to go unnoticed if you're a woman. People often don't expect a woman to be a private investigator and when I started years ago, there were only about three female members in the Association of British Investigators.'

Sarah, who has run her own agency since 1993, says her work often involves tracing biological relatives, or witnesses, or defendants to road traffic collisions, or finding evidence relating to a breach of a non-disclosure agreement or uncovering fraudulent personal injury claims, as well as clinical negligence cases, blackmail cases and asset tracing. She's even investigated hate mail sent to a celebrity and reunited wartime sweethearts.

But when she submits her reports, she's aware the repercussions can be serious, someone might lose a financial payout or end up losing custody of their child.

'For me two things are paramount to my work. Firstly, confidentiality. All my work is encrypted and password protected, and everything has to be in line with data protection guidelines. At the end of a case, all personal information and files are destroyed, because I'm dealing with such sensitive information.'

'Secondly, I need to carry out a Data Protection Impact Assessment (DPIA) on all potential cases to ensure there's a legitimate interest to undertake an investigation.'

But for some parts of her job, Sarah's identity isn't concealed, and that can mean her safety is at risk.

'Often on the basis of my work, people may end up in jail, become bankrupt or instigate divorce proceedings. If I've been instructed to get evidence for these situations, the secrecy of what I've ascertained is crucial. If I have worked undercover, I may need to attend court and present my evidence, then I'm visible which can put me at physical risk.

She's had violent threats and still has a scar on her arm from a knife attack. Her home is protected by alarms, cameras and top-of-the-range locks.

'I've had so many different undercover jobs, working within a company environment, working in entertainment or the health sector, working in the UK and abroad. Sometimes it is dangerous, and you've got to blend in to obtain the evidence.'

Being able to work undercover isn't the only skill Sarah needs to excel in her professional capacity.

'Some of the skills you need can't be taught. You need to be street smart for a start. I'm naturally observant too, which is important. You need really good attention to detail and retention for speech, writing and visuals. You also need to be compassionate, kind and sensitive to the different types of clients that want your services.'

'Some people work as 'super recognisers' and their retentiveness to visuals is mind boggling. These people work with the police to recognise suspects in a crowd, even if they have masks on and hoodies up. They can see how certain people walk or stand in an individual way. They haven't learnt this somewhere, it's a skill they have.'

'There are many types of specialists who are instructed, for example, fingerprint experts, DNA laboratories, psychological profilers, and graphologists, all of whom can add immense value to an ongoing investigation with their skillsets.'

'Gut instinct and body language are also skills needed for investigations. I can tell when people are lying. I might not know exactly what they are lying about, but I know there is a lie to decipher in some part of the conversation.'

'I also acted from a young age and went to drama school; I got adept at using all sorts of dialects and accents. Actors are able to immerse themselves in a role and finish their performance at the end of an evening, however with undercover work, although it's similar, the performance could last for days or weeks. It is totally exhausting.

'I think I'm able to take on this kind of work due to the combination of a drama background and being the sort of person that has good attention to detail.'

'Perhaps it's a bit of nature and nurture? The more you work in the environment, the more confidence you have in being able to go undercover and retain information, and not to worry about the danger and focus on the task in hand. You can trust your gut because you've been in those situations before, perhaps you are developing your skillset, teaching yourself.'

'It can be an intuitive job too, and you need to understand human nature, a pattern of life. If I need to speak to someone, I need to catch them at home. If I know a little about what they do for a living or their daily routine, then I can anticipate the best time to attend.'

Over the years, Sarah and the nature of her industry, have changed. But her ethics remain the same.

'I'm many years down the line now, taking on more corporate work and less domestic work. My clients are mainly solicitors and embassies. The industry has developed and there's an understanding about the effects your reports can have. The legalities mean I can't just look into a husband's finances on his wife's request. There has to be a legitimate reason, and a risk assessment.'

'Sometimes cases involve parents who may disapprove of their child's partner, however if that child is over 18, then they have a right to privacy. And I may decline the case. Again, it is also important to understand the implications and consequences for the parents, should their child discover a parent has hired a private investigator to spy on them. This is a big risk to a parent-child relationship.'

'Some people are very vulnerable when they come to me, and sometimes they don't know where to turn. I might not take on the case but instead suggest they look for counselling first, or head to Citizen's Advice or approach a solicitor. I probably turn down seven out of 10 cases.'

'Our industry is built on discretion, confidentiality, and of course responsibility to yourself and the client.'

CHAPTER 7

The Magic Circle and Freemasonry

'There are still many reasons to keep the method of magic secret.'

Laura London, 41, is the Chair of The Magic Circle Council, the British society dedicated to promoting and advancing the art of magic.

The Magic Circle started in 1905 at a time when magicians topped the bill at every theatre, and watching a magic show was as popular as going to a gig or the cinema is today. The Egyptian Hall in London's Piccadilly had become known as 'England's Home of Mystery', regularly staging illusions but it was demolished for housing in that same year.

Today the organisation boasts just over 1,800 members worldwide.

And while it's not a secret society in the true sense, with its Latin motto 'Indocilis privata loqui' translating to 'Not apt to Disclose', it remains a society that keeps secrets.

Laura says that many of the members would like to change the secretive reputation The Circle has, opening up the HQ in London for more visitors (you can already visit the HQ near Euston for shows and talks).

'Magic has been around for hundreds of years, the first book on it was written in 1584. The author Reginald Scott wrote it to show the method of magic to prove witches weren't summoning the devil when they performed tricks,' says Laura.

'And The Magic Circle has a vast library with just under 13,000 books of secrets in it, so while we are an industry that keeps secrets, the books show we still can't help but write about them!'

It's not only books that can teach you the basics about magic in the 21st century, however.

'Today of course, it's easy to access the secret of a magic trick if you go online or find a book, but to really understand the methodology you have to work hard and practice. And then there's the performance element of magic, we use misdirection and psychology for even a simple trick, let alone a complex one. Everything that surrounds magic makes it what it is. Presentation is as important, if not more so, than the method itself.'

'Within The Magic Circle we teach tricks to magicians and members, we hold workshops, and we run a Young Magicians Club (YMC). We teach magic very openly to people who really want to learn it.'

'But it's very hard to keep the secrets of magic today, we're in a new world, with the internet and some people are happy to go onto to YouTube and reveal tricks, they just don't care. And they do it for likes and followers.'

'However, lots of professional magicians like me still feel keeping the mystery of magic alive is important and entertaining, it means the audience can enjoy it for what it is, not knowing how it works.'

Laura is happy to pass on her secrets to those who are committed to magic, and when it could bring a little sparkle into someone's life too.

'Another way I pass on the secret of magic is through an organisation called Breathe, teaching the performance of magic as a fun therapy for young people who have a condition called hemiplegia, which is caused by brain damage and causes paralysis on one side of the body, meaning that one of their hands is weaker than the other and has difficulty with fine motors skills.'

'Traditional occupational therapy can be boring for kids, but learning to perform a trick on our intensive 'magic camp' helps these young magicians learn to grip and hold things. Participants can go from not being able to tie their shoelaces when they arrive, to tying them by the end of the camp.'

'At the beginning of the camp they have to take an oath not to tell any of the secrets of magic. And you can see why; if they then go on to perform the trick for others, which improves their confidence, it's important no one else knows how it's done. Keeping secrets in magic protects the performer too.'

Learning magic is a very special experience for many, including Laura herself.

'I discovered magic when I was eight years old when I saw my first magician. I'd had what we'd now recognise as an ADHD diagnosis and the doctor encouraged my mum to let me pursue anything creative that ignited passion, thinking I'd find school harder.'

'My mum owned a popular 80s nightclub and so knew a few magicians; the idea didn't seem silly to her when I said I wanted to learn magic. I'd spend all my money on magic tricks, particularly at Davenports, which was a brilliant magic shop hidden in an underground shopping arcade near Charing Cross station.

'Betty Davenport, granddaughter of the founder Lewis Davenport, used to serve me and show me tricks, only later did I realise she was one of the only women around'.

'I knew all about The Magic Circle and wanted to join, so I joined the YMC, and then took the entrance exam on my 18th birthday and became the youngest female to pass.'

But the society hasn't always had a female membership.

When The Magic Circle was formed, there were several highly regarded and popular female magicians. These included Anna Eva Fay, famed for ghostly manifestations and 'Mercedes Talma', whom Houdini dubbed the greatest sleight-of-hand artist he had seen.

She was also the wife of Servais Le Roy, who chaired the Circle's very first meeting. Interestingly, however, the organisation didn't admit women until 1991.

'They were feisty, brilliant and talented women, and revered, and it doesn't make a lot of sense why the decision was taken not to allow them to join The Magic Circle, so it's possible that they didn't want to join this new boys' club,' says Laura.

But as a new member, when she visited the first time and felt out of place, it was a woman who encouraged Laura to stick at it. The woman smoking a cigarette outside turned out to be Fay Presto, a magician famed as the 'Queen of close-up'.

'I was so lucky, from then on Fay took me under her wing and she became my mentor, taught me how to perform magic and how to entertain. After that I became part of the furniture at the club, and I have been ever since.'

Now Laura estimates about five per cent of The Magic Circle membership is female, with the YMC having about 15 per cent female members.

'So, we've probably got more females than any other similar magic club in the world.'

When she became chair in 2024, it was important for Laura that the Circle righted a past wrong. At the very first meeting that females were allowed to attend, The Magic Circle expelled Sophie Lloyd, who had successfully posed as a male magician and was accepted into the club as Raymond Lloyd earlier that year.

As chair, 34 years later, Laura tracked down Sophie to offer an official apology and a certificate of membership, this time in her own name.

Sophie's ruse was quite the story! Coached by magician Jenny Winstanley, Sophie Lloyd had posed as a young man in glasses and gloves, making a £5 note burst into flames and then reappear.

The judging panel was happy with 'Raymond's' 20-minute performance at a working men's club, and Sophie even stayed in character after she'd passed the test, sitting down for a pint with one of the examiners afterwards, and spending another hour and a half in his company without him suspecting her deception. Sophie then continued to happily perform as Raymond around the country until the group voted to allow women in September 1991. At that point, Sophie revealed her gender and was promptly expelled.

Laura says, 'When I first heard about what Sophie had done, I thought it was so inspiring. She'd gone to such great lengths to prove an important point, something the world needed to hear.'

'When I started looking for her, I wasn't expecting it to become such a big news story. It ended up in *The New York Times* and really captured people's hearts.

'Sophie was an actress essentially and performed as a little boy for her friend Jenny Winstanley, who was the magician. It had really riled Jenny that she performed at The Magic Circle but wasn't allowed to be a member.'

Sophie had to learn magic herself and worked to perfect her role as Raymond for eighteen months prior to her audition, wore a bodysuit and a wig made of real hair and face plumpers to give her a jawline, used gloves to disguise her feminine hands and spoke in a croaky voice claiming laryngitis.

'She didn't just prove women could perform magic tricks to the standard expected of The Magic Circle, she *was* the trick herself; she had the biggest secret ever.'

But it wasn't only Jenny and Sophie who had been outraged at the lack of female representation at The Magic Circle.

'It wasn't the first protest; in 1972 a woman called Diane Matthews had burned her bra in protest outside The Magic Circle's building. It was in the papers, but it didn't get much traction,' says Laura.

'When we found Sophie [in 2025], we put on an amazing night for her, with cabaret acts and magicians, the President, Marvin Berglas, presented her with a certificate, and it was a very special night. I'm so glad her story has been shared.'

The current membership of the organisation is now a more

diverse one.

'I love the direction The Magic Circle is going in, we're much more diverse and inclusive now. When I became chair, I wanted to give back to a society that had given me so much, that helped me not only become a magician but also gave me a second home and a great group of friends.'

'I want a building that is open, that is the centre of magic arts. We're an organisation that exists not only share secrets among our membership but we also have public shows and showcase our amazing collection and archive; it's a place of research and learning as well as performing.'

'The development of magic is a gauge of the rest of culture, the type of magic that becomes popular at one time, reflects the issues in society at the time.'

'A great example of this was during the war. A lot of magic made fun of Hitler, but that was very dangerous of course. There was a female illusionist called Ionia, she was British but lived in Paris, and when the Nazis came, she'd hide within her illusions.

'I believe magic is a gift we share with the audience and there's a sense of excitement about the secretive nature of the tricks we perform.'

Taking an Oath of Secrecy

'I can tell you I'm a Mason, but not that anyone else is a Mason, and that's where the secrecy lies,' says **Susan Gonzalez**, Worshipful Master at Universalis #21, a New York City Masonic lodge under the jurisdiction of the Grande Loge Féminine de Belgique (GLFB), a women's Masonic organisation.

'If candidates come knocking, I tell them that anything you want to know about Freemasonry, including the rituals, is online, but what makes being a Mason special is being in the space with other Masons doing the rituals, discussing philosophical and symbolic topics, going out and doing philanthropic work.'

'Secrecy is a touchy subject, many members of our lodge don't wish to be known as Masons, and so our oath to each other is that we will not reveal another.'

'Secrecy can be a double-sided coin,' she says.

Susan has been a Mason for over two decades and as a classical singer was first attracted to the organisation when working in New York and studying the symbolism in Mozart's opera *The Magic Flute*, which was greatly influenced by the composer's Masonry. When she discovered that the city had its own lodge open to females, she joined.

'I think what has impressed me about being a Mason is the lifetime commitment. It's not a club, and it's not like the church. We do not dictate what anything means specifically. It makes you ask yourself if you are truly a freethinker, you have some deep work to do.

'As an American I'm open about being a Freemason, although under the current administration I'm probably more clandestine.'

Viviane Barrois, the Treasurer at Universalis #21, is also a veteran, joining in 2001; her ex-husband had been a Mason, so she was familiar with the charity work the organisation is often involved in, and she discovered that her godmother was a lodge member too.

'You come to Freemasonry to work on and find yourself'.

'But first of all, we take an oath of silence and secrecy, and if I break that oath, I would feel like I'd let the order down.'

For Viviane, who is French, the history of animosity between the Catholic Church and the Knights Templar, makes being open about being a Freemason more complex. Historically, the Knights Templar was a military group that protected Christian pilgrims travelling to the Holy Land. It later inspired the Modern Masonic Knights Templar, a separate organisation inspired by their history and symbolism, that is an appendant body to the Freemasons.

'In France, Masons were persecuted, particularly under German occupation during World War II, and so nobody spoke about it. I knew someone for 20 years before knowing he was a Mason!'

However, Viviane believes the organisation will continue to grow in popularity, with women particularly, less because of the secrecy it involves and more because of what it offers.

'I think women need Freemasonry. When I visited a lodge in LA recently and spoke to the women that were involved in the ceremonies, they were diverse with different nationalities and different educational backgrounds, but they all came for the same reason, to work on self-improvement.'

'We have three lodges in the US: New York, Washington and LA, and one is opening up in Texas, but I think we'll grow in the future.'

Susan agrees, 'I believe we'll continue to evolve, with more female lodges rather than lodges that accept both men and women.'

Indeed, the GLFB is not the only Masonic order for women in the States; Le Droit Humain, which admits both males and females is also active. The Order of the Eastern Star is a related organisation open to women with Masonic family connections, but women cannot become Masons there themselves and cannot practise without a male present or be initiated.

'When I first joined, I was surprised, angry even, that men, primarily in lodges in the UK and America, didn't recognise or were completely ignorant of the fact that there were female Masons.'

'It upset me a great deal. How can you have a motto of liberty, equality and fraternity if you're excluding people based on gender or colour?'

'Women and people of colour had to form their own lodges, so my big hope and passion going forward is for all Masons to recognise each other.'

But there's an interesting myth about the origins of one of the very first female Freemasons, which journalist Kathleen Aldworth Foster used as the basis for her historical fiction book *Doneraile Court: The Story of the Lady Freemason*.

The story centres around Kathleen's family namesake (but not relative) Elizabeth St. Leger Aldworth, who was the 17-year-old daughter of the first Viscount of Doneraile, Arthur St. Leger Senior in County Cork, Ireland. According to legend, in the early 1700s, Elizabeth woke one night to hear voices and when curiosity got the better of her, she ended up spying on the Masonic ritual that her father, her brothers and other men from the town were participating in. When she was discovered, the solution came in the form of one Richard Aldworth, who suggested that rather than kill her, Elizabeth should be initiated, and he would take charge of her ongoing Masonic training (he also married her!).

After chancing upon the story and researching more, Kathleen decided to write a fictional account because 'the passing of 300 years and the layers of secrecy' that surround the story, meant nailing down the facts was impossible.

Whether the story is true or not, there's no doubt that women have been Masons, even if in secret, for centuries.

Susan agrees that women were known to have been involved in Freemasonry, at least since 1791 when Mozart composed *The Magic Flute*, as it includes female characters.

'The [Elizabeth Aldworth story] is an opportunity to give women's role in Masonry a start button, but I think there were women involved before that, and in fact, women have been involved in clandestine organisations for thousands of years.'

CHAPTER 8

Adult Content and the Professional Mistress

'There are advantages to keeping my work secret and it's mostly for my personal safety. I don't want anyone on a public site to know where I live or things about my personal life. That's how I think of the secrecy mainly, as a safety concern.'

Roxy Loca Amor is an adult content creator in the States. A stay-at-home mum with no source of income other than her husband's job, she found that the perfect side hustle was joining the adult entertainment ManyVids platform and earning money from home whenever she had the spare time. Her content is available at https://roxy-loca-amor.manyvids.com/.

There are over 100,000 other creators on the platform Roxy uses, and promotional tool Social Rise says that the similar platform OnlyFans, set up in 2016, has more than 4.11 million creators.[1]

'A few close friends are aware of what I do, but just in general, and none of my family know. My ex-husband was the only one who knew the information to my previous links, and which pages I was on because I protect that so closely. When we split up, I changed my stage name, and now it's just my fiancé that has that information.'

'Before I started, I did a lot of research on the various platforms to use; different ones take different percentages, but I also researched how to do this safely, and while the platforms have your name, it's protected from the users. You create a stage name and I now have a separate email, separate bank account and everything I need in that name.'

'ManyVids looks more like a social media platform, it's easier to find people. You can sell videos, pictures, bundles of things, items, you can have contests, and you can message followers and other models, which is how we refer to those that have their businesses on there.'

Is Roxy concerned that someone she knows in real life might spot her?

'The odds would be pretty slim of people recognising me; there are millions of people using the platform but I'm comfortable with that level of risk. I'm not worried if they were to discover it but it creates potential problems I don't need.'

Roxy started her work in 2018, after several plastic surgeries helped her grow in confidence.

'My husband worked long hours, and I started it as it fitted around the kids. I'd had compliments on my appearance, and I knew it was a way I could make money.'

'Over the years it's been a little bit of everything, from pictures with everything covered to specific kinks and fetishes.'

'A lot of what I do is acting and modelling. I'm playing a role, using a script. I've turned down things I'm not comfortable with.'

There is a sense of community among adult content creators, which has helped Roxy to grow her business.

'When I first started out, I asked questions and some people were really friendly, sending messages; they're supportive of tech issues and genre questions, for example if you didn't know exactly what something was.'

'The women especially are supportive of each other, they understand the problems because it's a niche job, you have challenges unique to this field.'

For Roxy, the secrecy surrounding her ManyVids career has nothing to do with shame.

'I keep it separate but I'm not ashamed of what I do.'

'I think it's motivating to your self-worth to know you can do this, that there's nothing wrong with doing this and that you can also be a wife and a mother, or whatever you want. On the site you can make adult content, but it doesn't change who you are as a person.'

Roxy also considers her work to be a body positive and empowering experience.

'I've gained more confidence, it's given me more of an understanding of who I am, and I've got more comfortable with my body. I try to get ideas from other content creators, and I've seen all different shapes and sizes, everything, all types of bodies. And there's no shame about it. It's more of a motivational thing for me in my day-to-day life to understand that all bodies are accepted. I am attractive, people do want to see my body, and it helps me feel good about myself.'

But she is aware of society's difficult relationship with women in her industry.

'It seems there is a double standard; plenty of men watch porn but if a woman is involved in any sort of pornography, then they're shamed for that. It's acceptable for a man to be viewing the content but not acceptable for a woman to take part in it.'

'The people that consume the platform, they're hiding themselves, and expect us to hide too.'

In fact, adult content creation seems to bring up many gendered prejudices surrounding the power balance and profit-making in the industry.

'There are a lot of men doing this work too, mainly for a male following, while the women-made porn is typically for male followers too. And as well as being judged more harshly for creating porn than the men consuming it, the women making content also seem to be judged more harshly than any of the men making it.'

'But I've gained entrepreneurial skills, I'm earning money, and I am in control of my career.'

Roxy has a teenage son at home whom she has to consider when she makes her content.

'I keep everything separate, and obviously my computer is password-protected. I also have a tote under my bed for all the props and materials. My bedroom is then code protected too and when I leave the house, I lock that door.'

'My son is now 16 and I've come to the realisation that if he found out, I would be straight up and explain it, but I'm not going to put everything out there on display.'

'Currently my son is exploring his own sexuality, he's geared towards dressing as a woman and going back and forth. We've had to be open on that, and accepting of different people and different ways of life.'

'We haven't specifically addressed porn, but I would be open to discussing it.'

And what are Roxy's plans for the future?

'I'll do this work for as long as I feel comfortable. I tried before to shut it down because I got busy, but it really didn't feel right. This work feeds into my creative side too, the day-to-day posts, captioning a photo, telling a story, or acting something out, it expresses a creative part of me too.'

'And this is just a small portion of my life, I'm not constantly talking about sex or anything; you wouldn't necessarily guess this about me. It doesn't change my personality.'

'It's flexible work, I can juggle my day and still do all the things I want to. When I have downtime, I can set aside money for myself or I can use it to buy things for my son at Christmas, just anything that I want, and to have that bit extra, it feels good.'

Her work has also allowed Roxy to become more comfortable with her own sexuality.

'I'm more outspoken sexually because of it. A lot of women are scared to voice what they want but I've found out different things just by watching others and doing my research. Things like using toys for self-pleasure, even clothing that I've got ideas from. It makes me feel more in control in the bedroom too.'

'I'm able to live a completely double life with my stage name and separate accounts and email. Really, I keep this secret to avoid unnecessary drama and judgement for those who are more close-minded.'

The Secret Side Hustle

Originally from Australia, **Madam Mayhem** (https://madam-mayhem.com/) is in her 40s and has lived in London for over a decade. She's used the five years since she got divorced to explore her sexuality, leading her to discover kink, start a sex, kink and dating blog and set up as an OnlyFans creator. She's also worked as a professional dominatrix (Pro Domme). This work affords her a valued second income and has helped her through periods of redundancy.

Madam Mayhem's Pro Domme work came when she was between jobs.

'My biggest fear is that I could lose my full-time corporate job because of what I do as a side hustle, as there is a huge stigma about sex work of any kind. And I think women being open about embracing their sexuality and being sexual, is very much still frowned upon, meaning that the majority of cishet* men have preconceived ideas about me when they learn about my other job.'

'I'd listened to podcasts, spent a lot of time researching and knew a few people involved in the industry, so I looked into hiring dungeon space. I also knew there was a shortage of dominant women available for cishet men wanting to sexplore their submissive side. I thought, I'm going to try it out while I'm unemployed as there's no risk of losing my day job.'

Mayhem has already had a taste of what happens when male colleagues find out about her sex work. It wasn't a pleasant experience.

'After I'd left one company and some people from work found out what I did, a lot of men I'd considered great colleagues, and they were all married with children, behaved very inappropriately. Right off the bat they assumed I'd sleep with them.'

She's also had men from dating apps report her to the platform they've met her on, once they find out about her sideline, saying that she's there not to meet people to date, but to look for work.

Like many women, Madam Mayhem was brought up not to talk about sex, and especially not the sexual pleasure a woman has the right to expect. Keeping sex life secrets has been a skill she was taught from an early age.

'I come from a family of avoidance. We don't talk about things, and we were never the type of family where I would have told my mum when I had early sexual experiences for example. I have sisters, but I've never had intimate conversations with them, we just don't talk about this sort of thing.'

'My sisters know I'm pansexual, and I told one about what I do, but she didn't ask any questions at all, and we've never talked about it since.'

'My family are on the other side of the world, and I love them, they are supportive and loving. But I'm the odd one out in the family and they don't know about Mayhem.'

'They've supported my decision to travel and live abroad, but they don't know about my sexuality; they assume I'm straight.'

'I've tried to explain that my happiness doesn't look like theirs, that I don't want to get married again, that I don't want to have children, but they wouldn't understand if I told them I'm embracing non-monogamy. We just have different views on how to live life.'

'I'm a relationship anarchist!'

Other childhood influences had also led Mayhem to feel shame around sexual desire and pleasure.

'I also went to a Catholic girls' school and that reinforced the shame around sex, and perpetuated the myth that sex is something you have once you are married to make babies. I've had to do a lot of work to undo that thinking.'

So how does Madam Mayhem keep her identity private, when the nature of her work involves a certain level of intimacy?

'My number one thing is that you can't see my face anywhere, including any of my social media pictures. And I'm so glad I did that now because AI and deepfakes are out there, which is terrifying.'

'I also make sure I get ahead of social media platforms that try and connect you with people you know, I block everyone at work and people I know from accessing my Mayhem accounts. When I start a new job, I go on to social media and find everyone at the company's social media and I block them.'

'I also don't put what I do for a living on my dating profiles, because I've had men track me down through LinkedIn before.'

Despite not being able to talk to her family about her second job, or to be open about what she does with her work colleagues, Madam Mayhem does have a supportive network she can confide in.

'I'm fortunate that I've made some good friends here in London, and also through dating as a pansexual. Some of my friends are in this kink and non-monogamous world anyway, and in things like the queer community, people tend to be more accepting and open. I've not had a single bad reaction when I've told friends.'

'Friends I've known for maybe 20 years or more, married friends, have even said my openness has helped them to explore and try out new things in their relationships.'

And in order not to find herself copying the pattern of silence she grew up with in her personal relationship, Mayhem is up-front with anyone she dates now. Her Mayhem Instagram handle is on her dating app profiles and she always checks first that potential partners are okay with her work.

'I want to be open from the get-go, and I tell them I'm happy to talk about it and discuss any curiosity they have with it. It also helps to filter out anyone with outdated, misogynistic views!'

'Women are raised to be people pleasers and centre their lives around men, and this shows up in the bedroom too. I spent many years living that way but in the last five years I've learnt to be more of an advocate for my own pleasure. After years of putting everyone else first, I want my priority to be me.'

Being open to communication is something Mayhem has learnt is necessary from the experience of her marriage ending.

"I was best friends with my ex-husband before we got together, and we are friends again now. But before we were a couple, he'd had an experience of being cheated on. This left him with a lot of insecurities, and he struggled with anything I did that made me look more attractive to other men, even buying nice lingerie, he thought meant that I would cheat on him too. While he didn't tell me to stop dressing up, getting my hair or nails done, I stopped doing these things to try and help him feel more secure in our relationship.'

'I had to suppress so much of who I was in my marriage and had to deal with repeated rejection when I initiated sex. He shut me down if I mentioned I wanted to explore anything and made me feel shamed for it. Eventually I just gave up, and we began to withdraw from each other.'

And what of the future?

'If you speak to any OnlyFans creator you'll find there's been a dip in subscribers. My peak was in August 2021; lockdowns created a captive audience. Now the economy isn't doing well, people aren't spending on extras and now with the Online Safety Act, online sex work is more difficult than ever. The censorship on social media is also becoming a problem; content that focuses on women's sexual pleasure is being banned, and there's a real disparity there, it's not the same for content that targets the sex life of men.'

Mayhem is referring to the Online Safety Act, passed on 26 October 2023, a new set of laws designed to protect children and adults online. It makes social media companies and search engine services responsible for the safety of their users in an attempt to reduce the risk that their services are used for illegal activity, and makes it their duty to take down illegal content when it does appear. The platforms are also required to prevent children from accessing harmful and age-inappropriate content and to provide parents and children with clear and accessible ways to report problems online when they do arise. The Act also protects adult users, ensuring that major platforms will need to be more transparent about which kinds of potentially harmful content they allow, and give people more control over the types of content they want to see. But critics also think it has a gender bias and that there is an element of over-censorship, particularly for educational content that discusses women's bodies or pleasure.

The New York Times has reported on the 'pleasure gap' Mayhem is talking about.[2] Typically, social media platforms will censor content and adverts related to women's pleasure due to policies that ban the promotion of adult products and services. This disproportionately affects businesses and creators focused on women's sexual wellbeing, for example those selling sex toys, while those advertising Viagra or lube targeted at men seem to slip through any restrictions far more easily.

'I talk a lot about the version of me here in the UK, versus the version of me back in Australia. It's very separate; I can be myself here, away from family and the people who expect me to live and be a certain way.'

'I've never felt comfortable opening up to my parents about Mayhem and that won't change. But not talking about it with a potential partner can be damaging. I won't go back to being that person who suppresses my own desires to cater to a partner.'

*Cishet refers to a person that is both cisgender and heterosexual. A cishet person identifies as the gender they were assigned at birth, and they're attracted to people of the opposite gender.

A Keeper of Secrets

'People come to a mistress to have a safe space where they can share their secrets. Sometimes I'll be the only person they've ever had a conversation with about these deep-seated and really strong desires, emotions and feelings.'

Rebecca, 44, has been working in London as a professional mistress and dominatrix for 15 years. Her work involves face-to-face meetings, clients visiting at her private dungeon space and going out to events and restaurants. She may also travel with clients and find herself staying in beautiful locations.

'It's a huge honour to have people share their deep secrets with you; there's something wonderful and rewarding when, in a short space of time, you're building trust and a rapport with someone, and exploring something that's so important to them.'

None of Rebecca's family know about her work however and believe she does something else for a living.

'My parents are quite religious, and I was brought up to be a virgin on my wedding night. There was a lot of shame and little to no education about sex when I grew up. If my family found out what I do, I think I'd be disowned.'

Fortunately, Rebecca's family lives in a different country and the physical distance makes it easier to keep her work hidden.

'But I wouldn't say that it's easy to hide what I do from them, because there's an emotional labour involved. And that's not something I was able to comprehend when I first started out. At the beginning, I thought it's just a few little white lies, but after 15 years, constantly having to lie is a weight.'

'But being away from them gave me the freedom to explore who I was, emotionally and sexually. I always knew I was kinky, but it took me a long time to grow the confidence and life skills that I needed to work in the industry.'

'I've actually come to professional domination quite late compared to others. But I'm glad that was the case because I think you need emotional maturity and intellect to navigate the situations and themes that come up.'

As a sex worker, there are lots of reasons to maintain secrecy over and above the disapproval of family or those that don't share your outlook.

'Generally, if I meet someone for the first time, I don't lead with the fact I'm a professional mistress. You just don't know how someone is going to react; there is a lot of prejudice towards sex workers. I also don't want to have to answer a million questions. It's not my job to educate people.'

'Secrecy is important for me, the agreement between mistress and slave is 'discretion is guaranteed and expected in return', discretion between me and a client is essential both ways, it's all based on trust in the safe space I create.'

'Keeping other people's secrets can be a lot to process though. My clients share their deepest, darkest, erotic secrets, and they can be relatively mundane or highly unusual. But they share the secrets with me when they don't feel safe to explore them with others. That's a responsibility I take on.'

'People can be really grateful and appreciative of this emotional transaction.'

Does the secret nature of Rebecca's work make it more exciting?

'Doing something perceived to be 'naughty' can add to the fun for many of my clients, and that includes making an arrangement with a mistress or dom in secret or maybe sharing their enjoyment of wearing lace panties under their suit on the way to visit me.'

'Since *Fifty Shades*, and with the internet and technological advances, bondage and discipline, dominance and submission, sadism and masochism (BDSM) is so much more out in the open. Before these sorts of things were subversive and part of a secret subculture. I do miss those days of working a little bit underground, it was more exclusive. But then it's wonderful people can explore their erotic landscapes without fear of judgement and guilt.

'When society does attach shame and stigma to kink, then people who enjoy that assume there's something wrong with them. They can spend a lot of time hiding that part of themselves and that takes emotional energy. When they are able to release it, it gives them so much pleasure and it's life affirming.'

'But secrecy is a double-edged sword, and the secrecy around what I do works both ways, adding fun in some cases, but making people feel ashamed too, so there's a balance to be found.'

'Another way people cope with the judgement that goes with kink is they compartmentalise their tastes. They find great safety in keeping it a secret and find it increases the pleasure of the kink or fetish to do that.'

Like many women, Rebecca finds space to share her secrets with close friends, who are there to support her.

'I think it's really important to have a place to unload my secrets. I have a couple of really close mistress friends, and we support each other. While we don't talk about our clients by name, we share our experiences and maybe offer ideas on how to progress. It's very important to have this, because you can feel alone in this industry. I also have kinky friends, who might not understand the professional side of things, but they understand the ideas I'm exploring.'

'Any partner that I meet has to also understand and be able to offer support in that way too. Some people would never consider dating a sex worker or a dominatrix. Some people get very jealous about the interactions you are having with clients, and what they think you're doing with them. It makes it very hard to date.'

But Rebecca is always up-front about her work with potential partners.

'It's very important to be clear about these things from the start, I don't want that level of mistrust or lies between a partner and myself.'

As well as being able to share her secret life with those closest to her and those she trusts, Rebecca also enjoys her role and the power she exerts as a dominatrix.

'I have this wonderful little secret of the power I wield, within an art form that I've dedicated my professional life to. What I do can lead to amazing moments of human connection. On the flip side, I can't always share my successes and it's two-fold. Firstly, to protect the secrets of my clients, but also to mitigate the judgement of being a sex worker.'

References

1. https://social-rise.com/blog/onlyfans-statistics (accessed Sept 2025)
2. https://www.nytimes.com/2022/01/11/style/facebook-womens-sexual-health-advertising.html#:~:text=A%20new%20report%20found%20that%20the%20social,citing%20policies%20on%20"adult%20products%20and%20services (accessed Sept 2025)

SECTION 3

PERSONAL RELATIONSHIPS

CHAPTER 9

Lesbian Lives

'I was so used to keeping everything secret, hiding everything, that it became the norm. I spent my life playing a role. And it destroys who you are.'

Maureen is now 80 and has been openly gay for 23 years. However, as a young girl she had no idea of her true sexuality. She was aware however, that she was different in some way.

'I don't think I had any idea of the concept of being a lesbian when I was young. I had a lot of male friends. I enjoyed being in a crowd with them but there was no drive to be sexually active. I thought I was just slower to sexually mature than other people.'

'I then fell head over heels in love with a man, and it never occurred to me I would be anything other than a straight woman.'

'But I never enjoyed sex, I found it difficult, it never gave me pleasure and for me there was a huge fear around it. I accepted that was just me, and I never thought any more about it.'

'I did know of people that were lesbians, but they were butch, and someone told me they used strap-ons and that was an anathema to me, so that put me off even exploring it.'

'For many years I was simply close friends with my husband really; we were not husband and wife in the marital sense.'

Sadly, Maureen's husband died by suicide in his thirties, leaving her as a widow. She then moved to a new area and started a new job.

'A woman I'd met kissed me full on the lips, and instead of feeling repelled, I was shocked and had this dreadful feeling in my body that I'd never experienced before.'

'It was only then that I realised I was much more oriented to have relationships with women.'

'But I remained very much in the closet. I worked with young people, and I was terrified of anyone finding out I was gay, and it affecting my job. Workwise, I feel ashamed to say if there was a big function, I wouldn't take my partner, who I was with for 20 years; I'd go alone. Despite the fact her family knew, and we had a big circle of friends who knew.'

'I didn't tell my family either. I just thought, after Mum dies it won't matter, I can just lose touch with everyone else. I'd heard lots of anti-gay things said in my family, and I just thought, I can't tell them.'

'Later my nephew, who knew, tried to tell my sister, but she wouldn't have it and insisted that she knew me and that I wasn't gay.'

'It was only when my partner was terminally ill that I had the courage to tell work, and I feel a bit of shame that it took something so tragic to make me stand up for myself. But I needed time off work to care for her, so it was for a practical not a moral reason that I was finally brave enough.'

'When I did, it was a huge relief not having to hide who I was, and a lot of people suspected anyway.'

'And I'm relieved I was pushed to do it because if I hadn't done it, I couldn't live the life I live now. I wouldn't have had the courage to meet Norah. I'd still be frightened little me. It's been brilliant.'

Norah, 76, has been Maureen's partner for 16 years. She too spent some of her life hiding her sexuality, at a massive personal cost.

'I realised I had feelings for girls, for my classmates, for teachers since about the age of 14, but I knew what I felt wasn't right. I grew up in rural Southern Ireland and was educated in a convent. There were no role models and, in an attempt to find somebody like me, I'd read the problem pages in my mother's magazines.'

'But I would never have actually spoken to anyone about it and didn't until I came out at about the age of 40.'

'My parents would have been horrified, and even when I came to England to train as a nurse, I was fearful and self-conscious if anyone mentioned someone else being queer or gay. I was worried I would blush and give myself away.'

'Sometimes as a nurse there might be twenty of us in the staff room, and if the lesbian thing came up, I would join in the laughing. I wanted to fit in, but there was real shame for me there. I thought I was abnormal and kept quiet.'

'There's been a separation between Norah on the inside and Norah acting, a disparity between what I was on the inside and what I projected on the outside.'

'It was an awful, terrible period.'

'I decided to just go out with boys and act the part, copy others, even though I never really connected with any males.'

'So, I ended up moving to the Middle East for work and met a man that seemed nice, and I just thought, if he asks me to marry him, I'll say yes and have a couple of children, and everything will be fine.'

'And that's what I did for 23 years until at 40 I met and fell in love with a woman and there was no going back for me.'

But keeping up the pretence of a happily married woman was a strain for Norah, and she became an alcoholic.

'Drinking was a way I felt I could escape from my head and my feelings, but it's a progressive illness and I got worse.'

'So, I had to make a choice. I could assume my straight role and drink, or I could live my life freely. It was a huge crisis point. I didn't want to go back to drinking, so I thought I'd take the consequences of coming out.'

'Now I'm the happiest I've ever been in my life.'

Coming out however is not without its complications. For Maureen her announcement came at a difficult time for her daughter who was 17 when she was told.

'She wasn't happy at all because it was a difficult time for her as she was on the cusp of being diagnosed as bipolar. Any change was difficult for her then, and she found it hard to be friendly to my partner for a few years. She also became a very devout Christian and so did not approve of homosexuality, despite having had a relationship with a woman herself.'

But these difficulties have eased over time.

'She isn't judgemental at all now, she's very accepting, she also adores Norah.'

For Norah things were slightly different.

'My family is very unconventional and it's likely my husband had his suspicions. My husband and I went to Portugal for a couple of weeks, and my daughter, who is also a lesbian, asked me, if I got a chance, to tell her dad that she was in a relationship with a woman. When I did as she'd asked, he replied 'I think I know something about that.'

'It took me longer to then tell him about my feelings. I prolonged the agony for a bit! I didn't know if I could do it or not.'

But Norah still suffered from her concealment of her true self, particularly within the religious setting of her childhood.

'You'd have to go to the priest, and I never told him any of these things, and it became just a game. But I had this fear and shame about all the parts of my character that weren't accepted and so I developed an ability to cover up. It's a skill you don't want, but I created a persona and played it to perfection as if I'd attended RADA. I developed a duplicitous nature and as I got older it got difficult as I knew I was not the real deal.'

For both women a lack of role models when they were younger was part of the problem. With no one to confide in about her lack of interest in a sexual relationship with a man, Maureen thought it was a problem just she had.

''When I was growing up in the Northeast of England there was no alternative to not being heterosexual. As a woman I was expected to get married and have children; there wasn't even talk about a career. At school we just discussed babies and cleaning.'

'Because I didn't know any other lesbians, and that it was okay to not want to have sex with a man, I personalised it and thought there was something wrong with me.'

'I lived with shame,' says Norah. 'It was very internalised, and the fear of someone finding out was too much.'

'I never felt authentic; it was hard to know who I really was. I was the person that kept all these secrets, and it knocked my self-confidence,' says Maureen.

'I know that it's taken me years and years to speak out because I was so used to keeping everything secret. It destroys who you are, really. I spent all my professional life in a role, an act.'

'It's taking all your energy to keep the lid on it, and then you've got no energy for anything else, to find out what you really like, to form close friendships with people. You feel you can't get close to this person because you're keeping a secret.'

For Maureen this also meant she missed out on making friends at work, people whom she could then see socially too, something she regrets.

'Friends would say they were meeting up with colleagues, and I just didn't do that because I wasn't able to be me. I've never engaged with people I worked with outside of the job. I've only just recently been invited to meet up at a regular coffee catch up.'

'There's a price to pay for keeping secrets' she says.

A Secret Diary for an Explanation

'My parents were part of the Silent Generation, and you didn't talk about your feelings,' says former family lawyer, and author **Helen Garlick**, 67, from Avebury.

'Part of the shock of finding out about my mother, was also realising that other people kept this secret from me too.'

The Silent Generation is a term that covers those born between 1928 and 1945 who were defined by the Great Depression and World War II. These experiences were said to have given them a respect for authority and a desire for stability, plus an acceptance of hard work.

Helen is referring to her discovery, that despite a long-lasting marriage to her father that bore two children, her mother was gay and left a part-finished memoir that disclosed this for her daughter to find after her death. The diary was topped with a poignant note scribbled on an envelope in her mother's somewhat indecipherable handwriting that said, 'I don't know why I'm different.'

As Helen read on, the memoir asked, 'I wonder how other lesbians cope?'

And on the surface, Helen's mother – and father – seemed to have coped very well with this divergence from the norm.

'My mum married my dad in the 1950s. He was a local solicitor, the President of the Yorkshire Union of Law Societies, and quite ambitious. I was born in 1958, and my brother two years later. We lived in a big 1689 William and Mary house with eight bedrooms and a billiard room. We had a pony paddock and a large greenhouse on two acres of land. We had other properties too and they enjoyed a lot of foreign travel together.'

And Helen's parents didn't lead a sheltered life either.

'They had a glamorous lifestyle, with lots of big parties where there would be openly gay friends, both men and women. They went to the theatre and set up The Doncaster Film Society, where they screened films that hadn't got certification from the British Board of Film Censors. They went to Royal Garden Parties, and she loved it all. Really, they were a Doncaster power couple!'

'Later it was an accepted fact in the family that one of her friends, Gwen, had a civil partnership with her wife, that wasn't hidden from me at all.'

Helen's mother was unable to finish her memoir as she died unexpectedly, six days after moving to a care home. So, Helen tracked down her mother's friend Gwen, and the secrets kept coming.

'When I contacted Gwen and told her mum had left this note I'd like to discuss with her, she replied saying that she'd expected this call all her life.'

'Gwen told me my mum had had several affairs with women during her marriage.'

'And it also prevailed that Gwen and my mother had been in a relationship too, and that they even ran away to London together when they were young. There they settled in a flat behind Harrods, which I thought was very much like my mother! Then they both got jobs and set up home.'

'But it seems my grandmother was having none of it and set off to find them. When she did, she told my mother she had to return home and 'stop these dirty deeds'. She insisted that my mother came back to Doncaster, to find herself a job and a husband. So, she did.'

When Helen first deciphered the word 'lesbian' in her mother's papers along with her partner, they looked at each other in shock and laughed.

'It was an absolute shock; she hid her secret so well. I didn't have the teeniest, tiniest inkling about her sexuality.' To her this was the moralistic mother who had told her she must remain a virgin until she was married.

'I think growing up I did know something was being kept a secret. If I came into a room of adults, everyone would stop talking. But I decided that I must be adopted and would rifle through my parents' paperwork to find my adoption certificate. It's hilarious because I'm a replica of my mother physically.'

'But I felt really strongly that I'd been born into the wrong family, and I was desperate to get away from Doncaster. I used to try to escape a lot as a child by taking myself off to be alone in the garden. I'd hide under a willow tree and read.'

'Now I feel that I was trained to be gullible; in our family we didn't talk about feelings at all, my mum wasn't warm or motherly. I've had to work to learn how to talk about things. And I don't trust people easily, I think trust has to be earned.'

But Helen accepts that her mother would have suffered too through not living the openly gay life she had wanted when she ran away to London with Gwen.

'I'm in awe that she managed to keep it a secret for such a long time. But I'm sad for her too. If you were a woman in your twenties in the 1950s, then you were incredibly restricted.'

'I noticed too she didn't call herself bi-sexual, so I think she knew her sexual orientation was just toward women. I'm grateful that she gave me life, but it must have been hard to have heterosexual sex when that was not what she enjoyed.'

'I think the pattern of secrecy in the family was pretty toxic, and probably one of the reasons for my brother's death by suicide in 1981, when he was 20.'

'And she and my dad both drank.'

Helen's dad died three years before his wife so whether or not he was aware of his wife's sexuality 'is the question that nobody can answer,' says Helen.

'But Gwen recounted a time when he, unusually, asked her to accompany him to the theatre, without his wife. The two of them watched a play about a man who discovers his wife is having a lesbian affair. Gwen said it was excruciatingly awkward, but that afterwards they still didn't actually talk about it! Was he letting Gwen know he knew, or trying to open up?'

'A lot of secrets have died with my mother and father, and there are a lot of unanswered questions,' says Helen.

In the memoir Helen's mother suggested her own mother had also been gay, which would mean she had also closeted that side of her personality too.

'My grandmother had a very strong personality. She got a scholarship at school and did a degree in 1919. She studied French and went to the Sorbonne, which was incredibly impressive for the time she was living in. She was also immense fun, if there was a party she'd be at the centre of it. But she drank too, to the point you knew you couldn't call her in the middle of the day because of that. But she also had very strong views and thought you should lead a 'proper' life.'

Helen's mother died in 2017.

'My mum was a complicated and somewhat manipulative woman. But she was interesting and interested in everything too. She adored the Proms, she adored music. A lot of my friends thought my parents were amazing. She did what she did but at the time it wasn't within her to be open about being gay. She was a product of her time.'

Now Helen has written her own page-turner memoir, *No Place To Lie: Secrets Unlocked, A Promise Kept* by Helen Garlick, with all that she has found out about her mother's secret life, and how it affected her family, including her brother's death.

'What I do know is that my mum loved secrets. And her memoir was almost her final big reveal! I'm glad she told me though. I'm glad her secret didn't go to the grave with her. For all I know though she could also have been a spy!'

CHAPTER 10

Secret Love Affairs

'I didn't tell my husband about the affair when I told him our marriage was over, I thought it would be too brutal. I think he may have suspected, but there didn't seem to be any point in aggravating the situation. I wanted to go out with some dignity for him. I only told one friend about it, who was very supportive. She'd also seen me and my ex in situations where she wasn't happy with his behaviour towards me.'

Sophie, 50, from the Southwest of England, left her husband after starting an affair. She's one of the 20 per cent of British adults who admit to having had an affair, although a third say they have considered it.[1] She's now divorced and still involved with her lover, who remains married to his wife.

'My ex-husband was very fun; he'd been in a band but became a civil servant. I wanted to keep the vitality of life, but he didn't. The relationship began to feel very misogynistic. There were no pink and blue jobs in our marriage, I did it all! I gave him a lot of chances, but when I left, he was devastated and shocked. I asked him how he could be shocked and said that he should have seen this coming. He admitted he wished he'd been a better husband and father.'

'We met at uni and we had some great times together, but we were quite vanilla in the bedroom, and I just stopped fancying him. I'd known the other man for many years as friends and we had kissed, but initially, I thought I'm not going to pursue this, I'm going to focus on my relationship with my husband. But my marriage just fell apart during that time.'

'My affair was a response to being ignored in the marriage. I got away with it, but then I decided to get divorced because I knew I'd be happier.'

Sophie's affair fits the research findings, which shows some interesting gender differences.[1] Over half of women who have had an affair have cheated with a friend, compared to just a third of men, who are more likely than women to cheat with someone who is a work colleague, a stranger or neighbour.

The main reasons for an affair cited by women were 'I felt flattered by the attention' (44%) and 'I felt emotionally deprived in my relationship' (43%). Men typically cheat for reasons of flattery (35%), but also because of dissatisfaction with their sex life (32%) – something mentioned by only 15 per cent of women.

Sophie was aware that her parents' marriage also took a lot of work:

'I know my mum had an affair, and that my dad was away a lot with work, and possibly unfaithful too. They often sent us away and now I realise they were working on their marriage, which they did successfully. They've been married for over 50 years now.'

'But it was an expectation then, to hold on to the marriage, it was considered the right thing to do, to battle through'.

But is a marriage that staggers on with both partners being unhappy really a success? Sophie isn't sure.

'I have friends who are so miserable in their marriage but the fear of taking that leap and being single frightens them to death. Sometimes they just toe the line and make him happy, but the marriage is horrific.'

'Since I've been divorced, I've told a few people I'm having an affair, and the judgement is there because this guy is married with three kids, and we've now been involved for six years.'

'When I was still married, we'd check into hotels and I'd say I was with friends. Right at the start I think it was an addiction.'

Sophie has plenty in common with her boyfriend but is also her own person.

'On an intellectual level we enjoy the same things, and the sex is mind blowing, staggering! We connect physically, intellectually and emotionally'.

'I'm about six years older than him but often feel that I'm younger!'

'I'm more liberal and a risk taker. I go to Thailand on my own, I have a need for exploration, I cook new things, but he tempers me. We both like to explore literature and arts, which perhaps we've not had an opportunity to do with others before.'

Sophie also describes how the affair had a positive physical effect on her.

'I lost 20lbs, my periods, which I'd had problems with, improved, I was full of oxytocin and dopamine, I became very driven to fit everything in. I felt empowered.'

'Now I've got my own place. I'm his sanctuary, he pops in, he doesn't stay over, we're really good friends, I'm a busy person and so he just slots around that.'

Being the secret 'other woman' isn't always easy though, but Sophie has no intention of being found out.

'It can be difficult for him to get away, and I don't want to put any pressure on him, but we make it work, and we message and check in with each other every day. First and foremost, it's a friendship, and it's still exciting.'

'There have been a few other dalliances for me, which I haven't told him about because I think that would break his heart. But I don't belong to him, and I don't know what he gets up to with his wife – and I don't want to know.'

'I have to be good at compartmentalising it and dismissing it, so I don't feel guilty.'

'I also make sure that there would never be any rhyme or reason for her to find out. I protect him and I'm very private, we're in a bubble and I don't want to burst it.'

'There was a point when his wife noticed he was using WhatsApp a lot, so we switched to Signal, which you need a pin code to access. I never phone him, he phones me, and I'm mindful of that.'

'There are rules on both sides, I have an older teenage son who is sometimes here, and I make sure they don't cross paths, although I've told him I've got a fella that sometimes drops by, so he will message before he comes over.'

'My boyfriend is not on social media either, which is really helpful.'

But having an affair does come with some limitations. Sophie doesn't ever spend a full night with her lover; a situation she's in two minds about.

'I would like to wake up with him, but he's actually never spent a night away from his kids. There's the chance too that spending the night together or even a weekend, even though I doubt that would ever happen, would change something in the relationship and take away some of the fun. At the moment we see the best of each other.'

'But he definitely experiences some guilt about any thought of leaving his children, even for a night. That's to do with his past. His wife does go away, and he does the majority of the childcare, he's very committed to his children and feels like he needs to be there and do his best.'

When Sophie tells people about her love life, sometimes other women respond very positively.

'I was at a black-tie event and got talking to someone. She said, "good for you, you're living the dream. I'm married to a man that snores, he's always moaning, doesn't get jobs done, I have to do everything for the kids. I might as well be single!"'

For Sophie her life remains relatively settled, having lived in her current town for a decade, with more than half of those in this secret relationship.

'These have been golden years, I've enjoyed it and it's a life of freedom. But in the future, I might want to travel more, and that would mean not seeing him for maybe six months or so. He'd be gutted, but he wouldn't stop me. I think we'd likely continue as it's a long-term friendship.'

'I've said to him if he wants to end it, give me six weeks warning so I can prepare for the next stage of my life. Realistically, it would be horrific if his wife found out, it wouldn't be unicorns and rainbows and it would change the status of our relationship. I'm not interested in taking on three kids, that's not for me. My next stage of life does not involve kids, particularly someone else's!'

'I'm quite practical, despite my enjoyment of the affair, the romance, the passion. If it broke down, I'd have to find my next thing and make it happen.'

Sophie thinks the secrecy of their relationship is part of its success.

'It belongs to us. Because it's a secret affair we don't have infiltration from outside, we don't get other people's opinions or dynamics, parents or friends commenting. I love the thrill of it still; it's a goal each week to see when we're going to see each other. I still get butterflies.'

'The affair is one of the best things I've ever done. It changed my life, my perspective, my appreciation for life. It was a sexual awakening, like opening Pandora's Box.'

Like an Addiction

'Because he was married and I was married, we were curtailed. We had to do everything behind closed doors.'

Diana is now 82, and lives in London. But in her 40s she embarked on a passionate affair outside her second marriage. An affair she says within which she 'quite simply couldn't help herself'.

'When something so passionate takes over, you can't think logically. It's only happened once in my life, and it was like an addiction.'

'I couldn't see the wood for the trees, I couldn't think of anything else but him whether I was eating, walking in the street, sat in a pub. I couldn't stop touching his head and his face when we were together.'

'It coloured my life completely and absolutely took over.'

'I did the most dreadful things because of it. My father had given me a lovely black raincoat, from Burberrys, I think. Well, I went to a pub wearing this raincoat, but all I had on underneath was my bra and pants!'

'I opened it up for a joke, and then I thought to myself, Diana what are you doing? But I couldn't help it. I was completely overcome.'

At the time, Diana was married to her second husband, a widowed man she'd met when she was in her thirties, while she was living back at her parents' home, with her infant daughter. On the day of their wedding, she was 37 and he was 63.

'My husband was never nasty to me, he was kind. He never told me what to do or laid down the law like so many men. But I never had any passion for the man. I liked him, yes, but I got married because I'd been living at my parents for ten years and I thought it was time that I left.'

'He bought me a nice flat, and we got on, and I was settled and away from home. In those days, expectations were less in a marriage.'

But Diana's commitment began to wane.

'I'd been married for fifteen years, and I was getting fed up with him. I know it's an awful thing to do. Our husband-and-wife relationship had fizzled out.'

Diana's husband owned a butcher's shop in Temple Fortune, where she worked as a cashier. A job she enjoyed.

'It was interesting working there, I saw life, and I got paid.'

After about 18 months of working there she got to know one of the other employees.

'I said, "Shall we go and have a drink together?" Then it started.'

The attraction wasn't based on physical attraction, although Diana describes her sexual awakening with this man as 'a burst of sunlight'.

'There was something so magnetic about him, he had such a

personality. I went completely crazy. It wasn't the sex, it was him. And it was the first time it had ever happened to me.'

'He was the antithesis of me in every which way, but I fell for this person. He was shy and not demonstrative. And it wasn't that he had huge shoulders or big muscles or anything like that, it was his personality and if a man's personality comes across, that's a strong point. He was the opposite to my husband in upbringing; and unlike my husband he liked going to pubs. He was a Cockney and five years younger than me.'

And how did the lovers keep their affair under wraps?

'The shop was closed on Monday afternoons, so we'd meet around the corner and go and have a drink or something to eat. Sometimes he would borrow a flat from a friend.'

'I used to come back late, maybe seven or eight o'clock in the evening, and my husband would ask where I'd been. I'd tell him I was shopping. But he wasn't daft.'

'Another time I woke up first thing and told my husband I was going to visit my father who was seriously ill in a hospital out in the country. I also phoned this man and asked him to meet up there. I drove hundreds of miles to the place, and it's something I regret now, and I just saw my father for half an hour.' The rest of the time that day, Diana spent with her lover.

Diana was aware that her husband had his suspicions about her infidelity.

'My husband actually told my lover that he thought I was having an affair, and said since we were friendly, perhaps he could find out.'

Diana's lover was also married.

'He once said he thought his wife might have suspected something. But he didn't want to leave her. They had two children, and they stayed married. She was very ill for a long time and then caught Covid about five years ago and died.'

Diana's affair lasted for three years, and for some of that time, Diana was single.

'When I left my husband, he was quite unwell, and I moved to Southgate, and my lover helped decorate the new flat. The relationship changed over the course of time, and we grew into being friends.'

'I was bereft of cash and so I went back to college and trained to be a painter and decorator until I stopped to look after my mother who was a widow by then and became quite ill.'

At the time of the affair, Diana told three of her close girlfriends. While they never passed judgement, they would ask her if 'she was off to the East End again?', where this man lived.

One person who certainly wasn't fooled was Diana's mother.

'When Eurostar first opened, I took my mother to Paris, and we stayed overnight. I phoned my lover from Paris when my mother was in the bedroom. She asked me what I was doing and said that I was ruining my second marriage after leaving my first one. She was very forceful.'

'And one day she walked up the road, burst into the shop and said to my husband, "I think your wife is doing things she shouldn't be doing" – that was a close one!'

Diana's father however wasn't privy to the secret.

Diana hadn't had a sheltered life before her marriage. She had lived rather an exciting life in Paris with her first husband whom she had married when she was 22. They had met in London and Diana found him charming. Prior to getting married she'd had a career in fashion design, also working in the trade in Paris when the couple moved there.

But her husband's character started to worry Diana.

'While I'd come from a home where everyone was kind and spoke nicely to each other, I found he became quite dictatorial. He started to ask why the way I organised the cupboards wasn't as good as the way his mother did it!'

'He's not for me, I thought, and I loaded the baby in the big pram my mother had given me, headed to the Gare du Nord, got on a train and left.'

'A lot of women find it difficult to leave their husband, because they have nowhere to go. But I had somewhere to go. I got back to London and knocked on my parents' door and I was home. Although at 27 or 28, I really shouldn't have burdened them!'

'I was also very homesick in Paris.'

Looking back on her affair now, Diana says, 'It was something so, so, wonderful to have experienced such passion for a man.'

But she is not without feelings of remorse about her behaviour.

'Now I'm in my latter years, I think really it was wrong to be unfaithful, maybe I'm old-fashioned to think that. I didn't even think about my husband while this was going on.'

While their romantic relationship came to an end, Diana and her lover became lifelong friends.

'We speak on the phone, occasionally meet; our relationship is not the same due to age etc, I hope to see him in a couple of weeks' time, for lunch or tea.'

My Dad Doesn't Know

'It's hard for me keeping my boyfriend secret because I battle with the guilt from not telling my dad and also struggle to be present when I'm on a date.'

Maryam, originally from Manchester, is a 19-year-old student studying Engineering at university. Her parents are British Indian, her father was born in England, her mother was born in India, and their marriage was arranged by their families. She has been seeing Charlie, who is white British, for six months, after originally meeting him when he was the year above her at college. But she has yet to tell her father, or her wider family including her grandparents, about the relationship.

'I told my mum a few months ago, she'd put two and two together. I had tried to give hints, and she could see I was really invested in the conversations we were having about dating. She asked me why I cared so much and if I had someone.'

Prior to confessing to her mum, Maryam had relied on using

her large circle of friends as a cover story for seeing Charlie. She even sent flowers he gave her home with a close girlfriend rather than take them home.

'I'd reel off a few names my parents were familiar with, and then add in a few others including Charlie's, to throw them off the scent.'

But concealing what was really going on wasn't as fun as it might sound.

'I'm actually so glad I could be honest with my mum so that I don't have to lie. I didn't want her to find out any other way and maybe be caught off guard if someone else in our community tackles her on it, if I was seen out and about with Charlie for instance. For Indian parents, it's a status thing if your children are doing well at school and behaving themselves.'

'I want her to be able to hold her head high and not be embarrassed about something I've done.'

Maryam's experience is not unusual for her generation and culture. Several of her cousins have had relationships with white people, often once they have left home.

'But I do have some brown friends whose parents are insanely strict, and it makes them hide even more.'

But as Maryam's relationship becomes more serious, being unable to tell her parents who she is out with means dividing up her time between her friends and her boyfriend.

'Because I say I'm out with a group, it seems like I'm always out with my friends, but I have to balance some of that time with seeing Charlie, so I'm going out more and more.'

But why might her parents disapprove of her relationship?

'It's not necessarily that I'm dating or that Charlie is white. It's more because of the age I am, and the stage of life I'm at. My parents see boyfriends as a distraction to my studying and success, they wouldn't want me to be heartbroken and fail at university because of it.'

'They know that I have white friends, because they raised us in a white community, they recognise a good heart more than skin colour or anything like that.'

'But they are protective and have no experience of a culturally mixed relationship. They worry that I might lose my Indian identity. At some of the schools I attended there was no diversity and at others there was, it was waves of culture shocks. I don't disagree with them about knowing my heritage, but I can't help who I like romantically, and I'd always want a partner to respect my culture.'

'My parents aren't expecting me to have an arranged marriage, in fact they are focussed on me working hard at university and getting a good career, rather than settling down and having children. There's no rush for me to get married. They'd want me to find the right person and not hurry into it and end up divorced.'

When might Maryam's dad be more accepting of her love life?

'I know the uni course I'm doing will bring financial freedom, and when I move out of home, I won't have a set of rules to follow.'

And what is the downside of keeping secrets, could Maryam be in any danger?

'I'm not too worried because Charlie isn't the sort of person to put me in danger, but plenty of my friends know where I am, plus Mum would know. I'd be more nervous if I was hiding seeing someone from everyone.'

'When I was first seeing Charlie and figuring it out and no one knew about it, it was quite exciting as I'd had a crush on him for ages. But as it's gone on and I've done things like meet his parents, it's got a bit harder.'

'And there are random things I worry about, like getting snapped on a traffic camera and Charlie being visible in the photo, so it's quite stressful thinking about stuff like that.

'I want to be respectful to my parents, and I don't want to make them feel uncomfortable but I don't want to break up with him just so they are happy. I just have to fight my way through this and see how it goes.'

Maryam remains conflicted about keeping her secret.

'It does break my heart a bit, because you want to tell your parents fun or exciting things.'

References

1. https://yougov.co.uk/society/articles/12404-one-five-british-adults-admit-affair (accessed Sept 2025)

CHAPTER 11

Kink and Fetish Relationships

'Honestly? It was delicious. I had this naughty secret that would have shocked my colleagues; there was also this sense of superiority that I was having this intense, deeply sexual relationship… and they weren't'.

This is **Sarah**, 62, a therapist who now lives in Spain discussing the BDSM relationship she had in her 40s, when she lived in London and worked as a manager in a corporate environment.

'At the time I had a three-bed semi in the suburbs, a dog and a lodger. As far as the outside world was concerned, I just saw my tax accountant boyfriend every weekend. What they didn't know was that he controlled how I dressed every day, and that I wore kinky underwear and a leather collar under my increasing number of polo-neck jumpers.'

'We kept it secret by presenting as a normal couple, albeit very intense, close and physical. We (especially, he) knew the limits of what we'd let other people see.'

'Looking back, I think if someone had been astute, they might have picked up on it not being a conventional relationship, but nobody ever said anything.'

Sarah also found it easy to keep the secret because she's naturally introverted, although admits the hidden nature of her lifestyle added to the fun, speaking only of her secret to friends that she'd made within the kink community.

Sarah became involved in the consensual Total Power Exchange (TPE) relationship after replying to an online advertisement looking for a submissive. A TPE relationship is a continuous power exchange, across all areas of life. The dominant has the right to make decisions in any and all aspects of their submissive's life. The submissive explicitly consents to this power exchange, although there may be pre-agreed limits.

While her partner had decades of experience, for Sarah, it was her first experience of kink.

'I came to it very late and was only into it for that relationship.'

'This was a kink that must have lay dormant in me for some time. I was looking for something alternative and I'd fantasised about it. I didn't realise this world existed, but I was like a kid in a sweet shop.'

'BDSM had excited me, but I could never really put it into words or explain it, but when this came along, meeting him was like birthdays and Christmas all coming at once. To get properly tied up by someone who knows exactly what they're doing.'

'I also got to wear some amazing clothes, I remember I wore these thigh-high stiletto boots to a club in Birmingham.'

By voluntarily choosing to give control to her dominant partner, Sarah was stepping away from her everyday life, and vice-versa. The relationship allowed the pair to explore a different dynamic.

'We both had demanding jobs at the time. In his job he had to abide by set rules, he was told what to do and had to follow orders, whereas in mine I was always in charge, responsible and had to tell people what to do.'

But it was also important for her partner to maintain their secret, because he was well known in his small community.

'It would have been career suicide for him for it to get out.'

'For me it was the perfect time to explore this part of my sexuality. I didn't have any family in the area, and no one knew me as other than the person I wanted them to see.'

'I remember reading that a small percentage of the population have a genetic predisposition for kink, just like some people don't like coriander!'

Sarah also says that at the time of her relationship, twenty-five years ago, sexuality of any type was far less expressed or discussed in professional settings.

'Since the advent of the book and film *Fifty Shades of Grey*, BDSM has become more talked about and mainstream, but at the time it was just one kink too far. Giving up freedom and taking orders from somebody was just unacceptable to most people.'

'*Fifty Shades* had a lot to answer for. I think it allowed people to discuss and experiment with games, toys and role playing but few realise the practicalities and intensity of a TPE style of relationship. There's a lot of responsibility on both sides but there is also complete openness and honesty. The downside of BDSM in the mainstream is stuff like choking and non-consensual anal sex. There are two vital concepts in BDSM; SSC, which means safe, sane, consensual and RACK, risk-assessed consensual kink.'

In the past, BDSM has been considered a fringe sexual activity, but more recent research suggests a third of the population may be incorporating it into their love lives.[1] Because the practice typically involves honest communication, it may even increase intimacy between partners.

Dr Lori Beth Bisbey is a sex, relationship and intimacy coach and psychologist. She was the specialist who guided couples on *Open House: The Great Sex Experiment* and is the host of the popular podcast *The A to Z of Sex*.

She says that in the past Christian beliefs have meant there is more stigma attached to enjoying sex as a woman than there is for a man, and that this extends to sexual kinks too.

'A woman might keep her enjoyment of sex, enjoyment of kinks and her sexuality secret for fear of being shunned, left by a partner, attacked in a variety of ways by those who believe it is sinful or wrong.'

'While it's not as common anymore for women to not embrace their sexuality fully, it is still an issue' says Beth.

Beth agrees that some people find secrets exciting, but that keeping an enjoyment of sex, and enjoyment of kinks, does not fit into this category.

She says, 'Keeping your true sexual identity secret can be harmful to your relationships as you are not present with your partner and lying in a relationship about things like this is inherently harmful to the self as it is hard to get satisfaction if you are keeping your desires secret.'

And a BDSM lifestyle can be more complex than popular culture might make it seem in that it extends well beyond the bedroom into everyday life. While it's part of the deal that the submissive agrees to surrender control, they do retain some sway.

Sarah explains, 'Yes, they give the control to the dominant in the relationship, but ultimately, they have the power to walk away and say 'no' or use a safe word.'

'Also, the dominant partner has a very precious belonging and it's their duty to look after it, to cherish it. You can't play with your favourite toy if you break it.'

But Sarah's BDSM relationship was not to last forever.

'It finished fairly dramatically, although we remained friends. It was too intense; it wasn't good for my mental health and had begun to feel abusive. It hurt like hell, but I walked away.'

'The secretive nature of our relationship was not an issue in the breakup, but I was losing sight of myself and my boundaries. I felt relief when I sent the message saying I wanted to be released.'

But the secrets she shared with her partner made it hard to discuss the breakup.

'Because of the nature of our relationship, it was hard to answer the natural questions people had when it came to an end. The kink community has a saying 'don't frighten the vanillas (those whose sexual activities are considered conventional or mainstream).'

It signalled a change for Sarah.

'Since I'd also got passed over for a promotion at work, I upped and left for Spain, living off my savings for a time.'

'After a while, I met a new partner, retrained as a therapist and began a new life here.'

'I look back on my BDSM relationship with great fondness though. It was a time of experimentation, excitement, deep emotions and pushing boundaries, but it was also exhausting mentally and physically. I'd do it all over again, just not now.'

'Today I live on a farm, without the stress of deadlines, targets, office politics and social requirements of my former life. The weather is my master now!'

The 'Throuple' that I'd Rather Forget

'People would be surprised if they knew the story, because you're not going to look at me and think 'she's a goer'!'

Melissa is 59 and lives in Deal in Kent. But she has a secret past that still makes her squirm in embarrassment when she recalls the details, and one that allows her in hindsight to pass on some wisdom to anyone that considers themselves sexually adventurous.

'When I lived in the city, I had a long-term partner, Ben. He was often away because he was originally from Australia. He'd go home for months at a time, leaving me alone in our flat and running our financial investment business by myself.'

Despite presenting as a very average couple, behind closed doors Ben was what Melissa describes as 'spicy'; he'd already slept with over 40 women when he met Melissa, and he made it clear to her he was keen to open the relationship up and go to swingers' parties.

'I wasn't really into the idea, but I would probably have gone to a sex party if he'd asked. I was in my thirties at the time and I thought I could try things, that it wasn't a big deal if everyone involved was safe. But this issue was always there in the relationship; he wanted to be more and more sexually adventurous.'

'When he came back from a long visit in Oz, I'd ask him if he had anything to tell me, because I wasn't keen for my sexual health to be put at risk. He'd always say he had nothing to tell, but then a few weeks later would admit something. One time it was that he'd watched porn with a close male friend and allowed the guy to give him a blowjob, and the guy had wanted him to reciprocate, but he didn't enjoy it, so stopped halfway through. Another time he confessed he'd been with a sex worker.'

Over time Melissa began to feel Ben's behaviour was quite unfair, as she remained faithful when they were apart, and his promiscuity was putting her at risk.

'An ex, from university, John, got in touch by email, and after a few phone calls we arranged to meet up. He'd always been a great guy at university, kind, but perhaps a bit insecure. He'd split from his wife, with whom he had a son, and I assumed he was living alone back up in Leeds. I didn't really go looking for a sexual relationship with him but somehow it developed into one.'

When Ben next came home, Melissa feeling terrible, confessed that she'd hooked up with John. But instead of being angry, Ben was pleased and wanted John to come and visit.

'Ben really liked the idea. He'd always wanted to see what an open relationship was like, but would have preferred to make up a throuple with a female and had tried to hook us up with a female friend in the past who had refused. But he was keen for us to be involved with John, who was coming and going to our house from Leeds, and that arrangement probably lasted for about nine to twelve months.'

'John even spent that Christmas with us, with my dad and sister visiting, and neither of them questioned why we had this extra man living with us, because we often had friends staying, particularly if they were visiting from Australia.'

During this time, Melissa began to remember just why the initial relationship hadn't worked out with John.

'He was a bit of a damp squib, and the sex was shit. He had a micropenis too.'

She also found the throuple arrangement exhausting both mentally and physically.

'If I had sex with John, then Ben would have to have sex with me straightaway. Basically, it always felt that one of them had a demand I had to fulfil. I stopped enjoying the arrangement pretty quickly. But it carried on. John had no reason to leave, and Ben was keen to continue this way. Although I had begun to wonder how I could get out of it.'

During the Christmas break, John left the house to call his son back in Leeds. At the time Melissa thought this was normal, after all with a full house who wants to have a phone call with an audience. This was before the days when we all had a mobile to hand.

'I started to realise John wasn't all he seemed when I'd paid for us to do some training together in Birmingham. After the training there was a ball in London, but rather strangely John wasn't planning on staying with us that night. I discovered while we were out that he'd become involved with someone on the training course. Of course I couldn't say anything to anyone there about it, because no one knew that we were involved with each other.'

For Melissa, John's new relationship meant the arrangement between him, her and Ben was now over, and it suited her just fine.

'But then I was asked to call John's wife for some reason, and from that conversation I learnt that since university John had become a real womaniser. He'd left her for another woman that he was still living with and was now cheating on her with us, as well as cheating on us all with the woman from the training course. He was basically a sex addict!'

But things were about to get a lot worse for Melissa. Her relationship with Ben broke down completely and he returned to Australia. There he developed serious psychosis and began a campaign against Melissa, claiming she'd ruined their relationship by having an affair with John and had stolen the business they shared from him. Ben's mental health became so bad he was sectioned by the police after he became dangerous.

Ben continued to harass Melissa by email, copying in many friends, staff and clients with his accusations and ruining her business reputation, causing an important deal to collapse at the last minute. He reported her to the police for fraud and to HMRC. Ben even uploaded a sex tape Melissa had reluctantly made with him onto the company servers. She was left humiliated and in financial ruin.

'I was being stalked and targeted by people he knew; I had violent threats, I did not know where or what he was posting about me, I lost all the properties I had acquired and was made bankrupt. It was a traumatic 18 months,' says Melissa.

And because Melissa had kept her and Ben's throuple relationship with John a secret, Ben was able to portray himself to everyone as the injured party.

'All this from somebody I was with for 13 years and who I thought loved me; he weaponised everything he could against me, and that included the fact I'd agreed to open up our relationship to a third person because he wanted to, but that we'd kept that a secret.'

'I don't think people would ever have guessed what was going on behind the scenes when we were together. We seemed like a regular couple. Ben wasn't into public displays of affection and didn't come across as a player.'

Looking back, Melissa has some advice for others thinking of taking their sex lives that bit further.

'My advice to anyone thinking about doing the same as me and Ben would be to really research your third person, make sure they are who they are portraying themselves as. Opening up our relationship ruined it, so you need to be on strong ground and really trust each other. All three of you need to sit down and talk about it openly and set the ground rules together. We didn't do that.'

Melissa's experience has had a massive impact on her life, not least losing her businesses and the financial security she'd worked hard to achieve.

'I still feel like I can't talk about the true nature of our relationship because you are judged as a woman doing this. If I was to say

I'd brought a third person into a relationship and it went horribly wrong, people would say I'd got what I deserved.'

'There are a lot of double standards still, especially if you're a business owner. I did Tantric training, but I'd never tell anyone about that either. Look at the publicity Sting got when he claimed he had seven-hour Tantric sex marathons.'

'I'd have to know someone really well before I told them about my past, my current partner who I've been with for 12 years knows, as we have a very honest relationship, although I haven't gone in to too great a detail. And my dad and my sister know, and they also know I'm embarrassed about it too! In fact, my sister and my partner will bring it up to tease me occasionally, because they know my reaction will be to cringe!'

References

1. https://www.psychologytoday.com/gb/blog/all-about-sex/202301/bdsm-is-increasingly-mainstream-and-it-boosts-intimacy (accessed Sept 2025)

CHAPTER 12

Hypersexuality as a result of Incest

'I've lived my whole life with hypersexuality and compulsive sexual behaviours, with several episodes of dark, invasive, violent fantasies about killing my father. Of course, they are related.'

Bea, 52, London, is a survivor of incest. Her biological father is a three-time convicted child sex offender with an offending history that goes back four decades. His first court case, related to her, was in 1983, when he pleaded guilty to multiple charges spanning several years, and received two years of probation and an order to see a psychiatrist.

'I've always been vocal about the abuse, but my hypersexuality as a result of it, that I've never talked about, that's what I've tried to keep hidden.'

'I grew up in the Mormon church in Hampshire,' says Bea, 'The abuse happened against the backdrop of that religion. I didn't get out of that religious cult until I was in my mid-thirties.'

'My mother had severe postnatal depression; she had four children under the age of five. The first ten years of my life were very traumatic.'

'My mother was being horrifically abused by my father and raped by him too. She reached out for help many times, to her

GP, to the police, to social services. Their solution to all this was to have my baby sister adopted and to get her a job so she was out of the house more.'

'Just before my fourth birthday, my mother walked out. I think the incestuous sexual abuse started then, as I was left in the sole care of my father, but it could have started earlier.'

'Sexual abuse in the first five years of your life lays down your neurobiological architecture and attachment style, so it was almost inevitable that I would develop disordered sexuality.'

'We had lots of nannies and babysitters, and other girls came from the church to help, and my father taught guitar to children, too. He was later excommunicated from the church, so I suspect there were complaints and young girls involved.

'I was 11 when my father was arrested. When he walked out of court, a free man, I knew nothing about it. I was told to try to put the past behind me.'

But Bea's sexual abuse in infancy had left its mark.

'I was 13 when I started having sex with the boy next door and giving him blowjobs. I was also raped when I was babysitting on the council estate where we lived. The couple came back drunk from a night out, and when she went off to bed, he came and raped me, but it didn't feel like rape to me, because in my mind, that is just what happens. I just thought, I know what I have to do here, he wants sex from me, I know how to do that. I was 13, he was probably in his 30s.'

'My mum was really worried about me having sex, so she put me on the pill. I think she knew it was because of the sexual abuse. Her priority was to protect me from getting pregnant.'

'I became the go-to person among my peers for sex questions because I had all this experience and knowledge, and I was very open about it.'

'I had sex with anyone who gave me attention; it was a compulsion. If I got close to anyone, I would automatically want to be sexual with them.'

'All through my teenage years, I was having really unsafe sex, rarely with a condom, with all kinds of men, often ending up at theirs and not knowing where I was.'

'Looking back with the wisdom I have now, I can see I sought attachment, connection and attention through sex.'

'I don't think the prevalence of hypersexuality among women who have been abused at a young age is understood or acknowledged.'

'We used to call women like me nymphomaniacs. Women like me often become sex workers, or today, it would be OnlyFans, and then we are shamed all over again, whilst someone in the background gets richer, commodifying our sexual trauma; human sex dolls, programmed to be sexually available whenever activated.'

Bea says that compulsive sexual behaviour or hypersexuality is not in the Diagnostic and Statistical Manual of Mental Disorders (DSM), the publication of the American Psychiatric Association used to diagnose mental health conditions. It provides a standard classification of mental disorders and is used by healthcare professionals across the world.

'And there isn't much research around females with this disorder either, it's all aimed at men and their porn addiction and compulsive behaviour, but this condition manifests differently in women.'

'My sexual behaviour was giving me some sense of validation because that was the only way I had got attention from my dad as a child. As I got older, I'd go out on my own to a pub, I would give off sexual availability energy, but not dress slutty, I wouldn't be overt about it. But every interaction, every male friend I had, even female friends, I would sexualise. It felt like I was getting some energy; it was fuelling me in some way. But then afterwards I would feel so ashamed and disgusted with myself.'

'It would get to the point where I'd leave jobs, change my circle of friends, and start over again somewhere else.'

'There was a phase where it was a different man every weekend, and sometimes I would throw up afterwards, out of self-disgust and go into a deep depression. And because I was depressed, I'd go out and look for another hit, another 'oxytoxic' bonding session.' By 'oxytoxic' Bea means the unhealthy behaviours, patterns and situations she sought out were toxic but connected to her need for a hit of oxytocin, often called 'the love hormone'.

'I would try to control myself and not do it, in the same way an alcoholic tries not to drink.'

'I wasn't in the church at this point, and I met my husband in a nightclub and thought he'd be fun to have sex with, so I went back to his house, but he turned down sex and said I want to respect you and get to know you, and I was like – what? Everyone wants to have sex with me, I'm irresistible.'

'So, we got together, and I was very much in love and got pregnant. When I became a mum, I was worried about being a good parent, so I rejoined the Mormon church, thinking it was a nice place for families, with singing etc and I got pulled back in. Me and my husband separated soon after that because he said I had changed, and we weren't aligned anymore. He was drinking heavily, he hit me once after I'd come back from church, so I left, and after that, even though I was in the church, I fell back into my compulsive sexual behaviour again.'

Bea says that at this time she identified with and modelled herself on the character Samantha from *Sex and the City*. She feels the TV series glamourised Samantha being so sexually open and suggested it was a kind of empowerment. But Bea says for her, her sexual behaviour was masking so much more.

'I didn't think for one minute that this was a compulsion then, I just thought this is how it is for sexually open women.'

Bea remarried, this time to someone from within the church community, where sex before marriage isn't allowed. The relationship lasted for a decade, during which she was faithful until towards the end when the marriage became suffocating.

'My husband typically wanted sex every couple of days. I had three small children, was exhausted, and struggling with my mental health. I started exploring kink and BDSM, and was very open about it with my husband, but he couldn't understand or support my explorations. Looking back now, I was obviously trying to figure out my sexuality, looking at the power dynamics within sex.'

'When I left him, I went straight back to my compulsive behaviour. I think my worst point was three different men in one week, and then I got into Sex and Love Addicts Anonymous (SLAA).'

Hypersexuality has also prevented Bea from finding a supportive female network.

'Because of the crippling shame I've lived with, I've struggled to build friendships, particularly with women, as I haven't found refuge there.'

'I also recognised that women didn't like me, I was a threat, they could see how sexually available and open I was, and how poor my boundaries were, how much I enjoyed male attention. Even though I couldn't see it myself, they could see it and sense it.'

'I never slept with a friend's boyfriend; I was more the type to go out and get chatting to a nice-looking guy. I had a specific type: good looking, muscular, hyper male if you like.'

'I got a real kick out of being able to get the hottest guy in bed, thinking, mistakenly, that I was irresistible and that it proved my value and worth.

Alongside Bea's hypersexuality, came another focus.

'When I became a mother, it suddenly occurred to me that my father must be out in the community and that since he offended before the creation of the sex offenders register [the police-managed database where individuals convicted or cautioned for certain sexual offences must report and update their personal details], he might be off the radar. But I knew he'd still be abusing.'

It took a lot of work on Bea's behalf, but she eventually discovered that he was back in prison, this time serving a ten-year sentence.

'When I knew he was in prison, it was probably the best I've ever been in terms of my mental health.'

'As an adult I've had contact with my dad just a few times, once in my 20s after therapy, and another time was in 2019, in my 40s when it occurred to me I'd not be told if he died, so I found out where he lived and knocked on his door and he invited me in to have tea and Jaffa Cakes.'

'All through this period, however, it has been very difficult to gain information from the authorities, as I'm not the victim of his later convictions. I felt the state wasn't protecting the public, and that they keep releasing him to offend again. The judicial system doesn't track the reoffending rates of serial offenders. I felt frustrated and saw him as a danger. And I started having these really violent fantasies about killing him and eliminating the risk myself.'

'I went to my GP and said that I was having invasive, violent fantasies about killing my father. I got some Cognitive Behavioural Therapy (CBT) counselling, and I think that's when I started collecting evidence and documentation, because when I'm working towards a solution, I feel better.'

'I see him as a risk to society, and I've spent the last twenty years of my life investigating him and keeping tabs on him. Gathering any documents I can, through the Freedom of Information Act, collecting newspaper cuttings and social services documents. I knew he worked as a porter at Park Prewett Psychiatric Hospital where he met Jimmy Savile. I recently discovered a photo of him with Jimmy Saville.'

'I also worry about the collateral damage of all his victims. My mother died by suicide, so did the two girls connected to his second conviction, as well as his sister, his cousin, and a girl from church, too. That's six women I would say are dead because of him.'

'He's in his 70s, and he's back out in the community now, after a third conviction. Of course, I'm going to want to do something. It's about feeling compelled to offend because the state failed to protect. I find it impossible to live in a society that routinely releases serial child sex offenders back into the community.'

'When the fantasies came back along with suicide ideation, the GP mobilised a crisis team, which didn't even get back to me at first. When the GP chased them up, they rang me on an unknown number, but I was scared to talk to them. How do I know they won't section me?'

'She [the woman from the crisis team] said if I wasn't at risk of harming myself or others that day she'd refer me to the community health team. That was six weeks ago.'

Bea is committed to her campaign to raise awareness and open dialogue about the way repeat offenders remain unmonitored.

'I've lobbied my local MP asking how they measure the risk of serial sex offenders reoffending, and how they decide who is eligible for release. Last year, a Ministry for Justice report said that their algorithm for assessing risk wasn't working. I got passed on to Lord Timpson, Minister of State for Prisons, Probation and Reducing Reoffending from 2024, but his reply by letter via my MP just fobbed me off and didn't mention anything about the chemical castration early release scheme.'

Bea is referring to a pilot scheme currently running in southwest England trialling the voluntary chemical castration of sex offenders, which the government has said it will expand. The scheme is designed to allow sex offenders to opt in to chemical castration, delivered through drugs, alongside a commitment to undergoing psychiatric treatment.

For Bea this is a hormone therapy dressed up as a punishment, whereby sex offenders might be eligible to get their sentence reduced.

'How offensive is it to victim-survivors that after battling to get a conviction, your offender can then voluntarily opt to have an injection in the arm once a month and get early release? This is not about the efficacy of the treatment or recidivism rates; it's about finding a solution for the overcrowding in prisons.'

'All I can do is keep on with my activism, write articles and post content on social media, so I'm not just carrying all this information in my head, that I'm putting it out there; so, I don't go and kill him.'

But Bea also found another way to heal from her trauma and understand herself and her sexuality. It also had a positive impact far beyond her own mental health.

'I decided to study sexology. I did a course in Psychosexual Somatics and it was the first time I felt I was allowed to sit with a group of people and talk about sex. Before I was always that person who had to talk about sex, like at a dinner party. Every conversation I had, it would turn sexual, it was a compulsion, and I couldn't understand why.'

Somatics is a practice that focuses on the 'soma', the body's internal sensations, noticing how it moves, feels, and holds tension. Psychosexual Somatic Therapy emphasises the importance of developing body awareness and connecting with physical sensations to understand emotional responses.

'When I started studying Psychosexual Somatics, it was the first time I could talk about sex with a group of academics who were seriously studying sexuality and all its facets.'

'It's when I came across the Wheel of Consent and started learning about boundaries. And then I recognised that I had no boundaries. I had no 'no', I only had a 'yes' response.'

The Wheel of Consent is a framework developed by Dr. Betty Martin to help people understand the dynamics of giving and receiving in intimate relationships. It is a tool for exploring consent, boundaries and mutually pleasurable exchanges. It encourages individuals to think about and communicate their preferences more clearly, leading to more fulfilling and consensual interactions. It helps those using it to tune in and notice what they want and where their boundaries lie. It also provides a language for communicating clearly with others.

'When I finished studying, I set up my own practice as an intimacy coach and partner surrogate. I worked with people who had what the manosphere calls 'low sexual market value' and I taught them healthy sexual expression using the Wheel of Consent.'

'I decided that the way to overcome the shame I felt was not by trying to change who I was. I realised that I couldn't change my psychological architecture because it had been laid down when I was too young. But I could employ those skills and talents I had obtained through trauma and monetise them and make a career.'

'They say that your greatest gift to the world is often in places you feel the most wounded, when you do it with consciousness, because you're not acting out.'

'I did that for five years and had a long waiting list. I specifically only wanted to work with people who were desexualised or sexually marginalised. I could see danger there. A lot of my clients were concerning; I worked with one incel [an 'involuntary celibate'; typically a heterosexual male who defines himself as unable to find a romantic or sexual partner despite desiring one, typically with hostile views towards women] who had rape fantasies and was suicidal. I worked with him for a couple of years. He's a completely changed person now and no longer has anger towards women. He no longer wants to rape women; he has had healthy sexual expression modelled for him.'

'Some of my case studies were extraordinary, one client was NHS funded.'

'There's a whole conversation about desexualised men, if they're not sexually active, and not sexually attractive, they don't have sexual expression, but they will find it one way or another.'

'This time in my life was one of independence, healing and purpose. But when menopause hit, I couldn't physically continue, I suffered from a complete identity crisis, crippling anxiety, brain fog and hourly hot flushes.

'I'm interested in how we can bring somatic consent practice into sex offender rehabilitation, as a treatment in prison; it's such a powerful practice. Why not teach this in sex offender rehabilitation? Consent is not a cognitive process. You can't simply say "don't rape" and expect society to change centuries of patriarchal programming.'

'It wasn't until I learnt to feel, track and speak my 'No, and have it validated, that I started to heal. Part of the reason we can't say no is because it is often dangerous to say no.'

'You can't respect another's boundaries until you respect, know and hold your own.'

Bea is now writing about her experiences in a book that will cover both her life story and the lessons she's learnt about sexual desire after trauma. She wants to pen a political manifesto, discussing issues like chemical castration, what's wrong with the current judicial system, and her solution to better serve both victim-survivors and offenders, including how somatic consent practices could be used.

'Despite this whole journey of hypersexuality, what's tragic is that even though I've had so much sex with so many people, with a body count in the hundreds, I can't orgasm at the hand of someone else.'

'Hypersexuality is not about chasing orgasm. If I start to go into orgasmic arousal, I will put the attention on my partner because for me, orgasming is traumatising. I think my father gave me my first orgasm when I was really young, and it was terrifying. Every time I approach orgasm by the hand of a man, I see my father's face and have flashbacks. Despite working so long to change that, I can't, it's just so deeply entrenched there, somatically in my body.'

'There is a misconception about women who are hypersexual, that they love sex. But it was never about the sex, it was about trying to feel deeply connected, trying to build strong emotion, trying to create an attachment with someone, and me thinking if I give them really good sex, they're not going to leave me.'

'I ended up leaving SLAA because the 12-step program says that you're not allowed any intimate sexual interaction outside a long-term monogamous relationship, and I recognised I didn't want a long-term relationship. I'd just got divorced for the second time, my kids were quite young, a long-term relationship was not right for me, but I still wanted that validation of a man wanting me.'

'I did do a year of celibacy in my 40s. I thought I was cured, but then I got into a relationship with a narcissist. And that's been a pattern, all the men I've had a relationship with were either narcissists, alcoholics or versions of my father.'

'Menopause was particularly difficult for me, because you lose sexual currency. I built my whole life basically on sex and sexual allure, as a way of getting through life. Everything that I did had some element of that, but finally I have some respite.'

But these aren't the only issues Bea faces as a result of her past.

'I'm 52 and that's the same age my mum was when she took her own life, so I have no reference point for living into old age. I feel a pull to end my own life, or that death is coming for me. It's like living under a 'death curse'. So, my focus this year is to break the pattern and survive. I vowed to myself that no matter how bad the depression or suicidal thoughts get, I will not leave my daughters, and I will not let my father win. The hero doesn't die; they mobilise an army and fight back.'

'My daughters have seen a lot of my compulsive sexual behaviour over the years, and it has impacted them. I think they hope I can move on and find happiness.'

'I've hidden these things from myself, just as much as others, because of the shame, but the last few years have been a time of deep reflection, and I feel it's important to talk about everything, because if I don't, I will never be fully seen or allow myself to be fully met.

'Shame is isolating, and I'm looking to change that. I really crave finding a group of women that I can belong to, where I feel welcome, wanted and accepted. Although at times isolation has served me well and kept me safe from other people's drama, I don't want to live hiding who I am anymore, in all my fullness, the mad, bad and sad.'

SECTION 4

BEING YOURSELF

CHAPTER 13

Witchcraft and the Occult

'I'm a baby witch because I haven't done a deep dive yet, I don't have an altar, I don't have herbs, and I don't dress like a witch. This is mainly because I've been hiding it.'

Lily, 37, from the Cotswolds, has been what she calls a 'baby witch' for a long time but is keen to progress.

But for Lily, witchcraft is misunderstood.

'The word itself comes with bad connotations but it's just someone who practises something more natural and works with Mother Earth, with ancient arts and practices.'

'I've learnt a lot through social media and through books, and in specialist shops talking to people. There are several good accounts on TikTok, that give good advice and show how to do spells.'

Indeed a few years ago the #WitchTok hashtag was reported to be more popular than those connected to the TV sensation *Love Island*, and to the hashtag #Kardashian, with over 20.7 billion views.[1] The trending content typically includes spells, tarot readings, seances, paganism and other occult practices.

American Teen Vogue also investigated the rise in popularity of witchcraft, and while we might traditionally think of witches as wizened old women in pointy hats, its piece suggests modern-day believers tend to be younger and more aesthetic.[2] The article shows how social media platforms including Facebook mean that those typically practising in isolation, can connect with others to learn and grow in confidence.

Lily finds the categorisation of witchcraft as 'dangerous' as odd, because some practices might be considered conventional.

'I'm not a woo-woo person, although I do have crystals all over my house. But I think they're quite accepted, celebrities are into crystals, you see crystal shops about and lots of mainstream shops stock them and even museums will have a crystal section.'

But she sees a misogynistic element to the negative beliefs about witchcraft.

'I think there's an innate sexism about the distrust of witches. If it's something that women do then it must be dangerous, we don't want them getting together and having their own special knowledge.'

So, what exactly does a modern-day witch do in her secret rituals?

'I do mostly candle spells, which means I have loads of little candles and follow instructions. I've carried out spells for justice, abundance and communication.'

'I've also tried cord-cutting spells.'

A cord-cutting spell is a ritual designed to sever unhealthy energetic connections to a person, situation or even a past belief. It works to stop draining or negative influences and to reclaim personal energy. The process involves visualising the energetic cords connecting you to the subject of the spell and then symbolically severing them.

'To start with you cleanse your space and your candles, and then you lay them out in the specified way. For the cord-cutting, you have one black and one white candle, a line of salt between them and a cord in a figure of eight.'

'I also do a lot of reciting and chanting and work with the moon. And I might have done a hex or two!'

And while Lily's immediate family and partner would be accepting of her interest in spells, she realises the rest of her family, who are Hindu, would find it odd.

'While I might tell a few people I'm close to, I generally feel a lot less judged by strangers. It would be easier to talk about it if I was in a bookshop reading a book on witchcraft for example. But people can't really tell, because I'm not walking around dressed like a witch.'

Lily has no plans to share her secret more widely any time soon. 'As long as I can keep it to myself, I will.'

'Perhaps the way society is structured means that women don't have power and control, whereas witchcraft has been handed down by mostly women and it gives you a sense of power.'

'This is something I do alone, I'm the sort of person who keeps myself to myself. I'm a homebody. That's probably why I don't make it obvious by the way I dress. I don't want people asking me why.'

'I'll do what I need to do for myself, and I don't feel the need to spread the word about it.'

Secrets from an Early Age

'I don't go around saying I'm a witch, but those close to me know I can achieve things like find them a parking space or get unwanted tenants out of their house,' says 54-year-old **Esme**, from Paisley.

'I don't tell people though because they judge. I've had people tell me what I do is rubbish, although my Nanas made it seem normal.'

Much of Esme's craft comes from a childhood spent with gifted and intuitive relatives.

'Since I was a child, I would just know things, and now, decades later I can tell things about someone just from shaking their hand. But I didn't vocalise it when I was a child.'

'I don't have an altar or use things like potions or lavender, but I tap into my ancestors. My grandmothers were both what they used to call 'fae', and my father too, but he didn't tell me until the end of his life.'

Although not everyone in her family was a fan of the beliefs and skills.

'My mother would send me to my grandmothers' because of their powers though; she hated it.'

'And while they taught me not to be fearful of what I saw and felt, my mum worried about my abilities and brought a priest home to talk to me.'

'But he'd spent time in Peru and seen a lot of witchcraft and other things. He spoke openly to me about it but told me not to tell my mother about it anymore.'

Another reason Esme keeps her abilities to herself is modesty.

'Also, I think it's egotistical to tell people about my gifts. If people come into my life and I can help them, I will. I help a lot of rescue animals because I can. Why would I tell anyone? I use my witchcraft to keep my friends, family, business and life as it should be. It's not that I don't appreciate my gift, I do, and my friends know what I am and will give me cards on Halloween and things like that but it's not out there.'

'I'm often just happy for people to think of me as a Feng Shui practitioner rather than a witch, as that's part of what I do.'

'But for me, witchcraft is thinking about something and making it happen.'

How did Esme hone her skills?

'It started when I was asked to go on a course to learn about becoming a hedge witch,' says Esme.

Contrary to popular culture, not all witches gather together around a cauldron, in fact a hedge witch doesn't belong to a coven, but prefers instead to work alone, practising rituals. Typically, this type of witch will focus on the spaces between the physical and spiritual worlds. Hedge witches are known for their connection to nature and herbalism and an ability to 'ride the hedge' between the everyday and the spirit realms.

'Witchcraft makes you very good at using what's alive in your brain, our minds are spacious.'

And Esme draws on lots of disciplines.

'I'm quite a modern witch because I use metaphysics, which explores what's beyond the purely physical.'

'One thing I do is knit, and with each stitch I think, I manifest, then I see a picture sort of opening up in front of me. But I'm also using Feng Shui, Chinese astrology, intention and manifesting in my witchcraft.'

'Through Chinese astrology you learn auspicious days, and days that aren't good. Then you can use the energy of that day to make things happen. You can have removal days, which is a great time to declutter, or a destruction day, which might be a good day to end something. I can use exact days and spaces to cast a spell.'

'Being in nature is also a big thing for me, being around trees, going to the woods.'

And it's not just humans that witches are able to help.

'I have a really good way with animals. I can calm them down, they trust me. A rescuer will call me to help a damaged cat become social again.'

Although there is a downside to being gifted.

'I can also attract negative energies, so I avoid negativity, because what goes around, comes around. I don't want the responsibility of triggering something negative.'

Could anyone become a witch?

'I do think my ability is a gift that goes through generations, rather than something you learn, but you have to train yourself.'

'And when you've been training for a long time, and if you're intuitive, you can achieve results far quicker.'

And it's in part this predisposition to being a witch that means Esme doesn't need to shout about her talents and beliefs.

'I have a lot of books about witchcraft, and people buy them for me too, but a lot of what I do, I do so naturally, I don't think about it, but others close to me notice.'

A Relationship with the Unknown

'One of the biggest things you learn when you first get into occultism is how important silence is.'

'And that's because you're starting to build your relationship with the invisible, the unspoken, the unseen.'

'You can't talk about it, because it can't be quantified in a way we understand now.'

I'm speaking to **Soror D.P.B.O.**, which is the magical motto name she has chosen. Soror D.P.B.O, 39, has been practising occultism in Scotland for two decades.

The dictionary definition of occultism is that it involves the study or practice of hidden or secret knowledge, often involving the use of magical or mystical powers, and the exploration of paranormal or supernatural phenomena. The term is derived from the Latin word 'occultus,' meaning hidden or secret. Occultism centres around the idea that certain knowledge and powers are not readily available to everyone and may require initiation, study, or practise to access them. Those who practise occultism explore the hidden dimensions of reality.

So, for Soror D.P.B.O., much of the secrecy she maintains around her practice isn't designed to keep everything she learns from other people, but rather a necessary requirement when exploring these hidden dimensions.

'The occult is a hidden force behind everything, it's intangible and unknown, and you tap into the secret parts of yourself. I'm looking to have a relationship with the unseen and the silence behind what is unspoken.'

'What I believe, can't be turned into something solid, its very nature is secret.'

But Soror D.P.B.O. is clear that the secret nature of occultism is more aligned with women.

'Women hold more secrets in general; they hold more things that are unsaid, unseen, unspoken. We're carrying much more around on the everyday, we have greater emotional depth, we see the subtext of conversations, we can see social anxiety people may be displaying. Women slow the words and spaces and emotions in between what people are saying.'

'These are the things we struggle to talk about, what it means to be a woman, and the social implications that have been handed down to us. It's become a burden of extra awareness but it's actually a skill and you need to build a positive relationship with that to be aware and go deeper into things. Women are good at reading between the lines.'

Soror D.P.B.O.'s childhood also allowed her to see that there wasn't one universal truth, as her parents came from very different backgrounds, with a contrast in social and political thinking. This means she was more open to learning to accept that there was more to understand.

She and her family also experienced trauma that wasn't spoken about, giving her insight into how often people hide their truth.

'There was so much that went unspoken, that I knew we weren't supposed to talk about. Everyone would say they were fine, but no one was fine.'

But Soror D.P.B.O. continues to keep her practice secret because the nature of the occult is to have a relationship with the intangible.

'When you choose silence, you practise it. And that's how you develop a relationship with the unspoken and the unseen.'

'And as soon as you put a name on it, it's not the thing, you're reducing it to just one example of the infinite possibility of what it could be.'

Perhaps the world is also not ready to hear about occultism.

'Now we live in a world where people are indoctrinated into this viewpoint that you have to show everything and be the loudest voice in the room, you have to stand out, put your whole life on Instagram and show how good life is,' she says.

For Soror D.P.B.O., talking about her experiences also comes with an element of risk.

'People don't know what occultism is, and they don't want to look into the nature of the unknown. So, they'll either reject it and say it doesn't exist, or they'll say you're crazy.'

'Transformation is painful, scary and difficult, you have to let go of things that used to feel safe. But you have to trust you'll come out of the other end wiser, you'll know yourself more and have the capacity to change and grow in any way you want.'

'Occultism does empower you too, which might frighten some people. When you tap into the truth of reality, then you're free from other people's meaning, and you're in a whole different place to experience reality from, where you choose.'

Soror D.P.B.O.'s practice is also very precious and were someone to try to put a label on it from the outside, it would be upsetting for her.

'The most painful thing about sharing secrets is if they've been turned into something that doesn't represent the reality of what they were.'

References

1. https://www.spectator.co.uk/article/the-rise-of-witchtok/ (accessed Sept 2025)
2. https://www.teenvogue.com/story/as-witchcraft-becomes-more-common-witches-weigh-in-on-stigma (accessed Sept 2025)

CHAPTER 14

Neo-Shamanism

'I wouldn't speak about my Shamanic practices, because the church isn't always accepting of such practices; it's more accepting of Islam, Judaism, Hinduism and Buddhism, the established faiths, than this.'

Despite being brought up as an only child in a small family with strong ties to the Christian church and later becoming a minister in her hometown of Manchester, **Patricia** also practises neo-Shamanic rituals including travelling on the drum, contacting ancestors and the use of trance. But this is not something she has always been able to openly embrace.

Shamanism is a spiritual practice involving a practitioner who enters an altered state of consciousness, or 'shamanic journey', to interact with the spirit world. Neo-shamanism is Shamanism practised by Western people as a contemporary spiritual practice.

'I wouldn't speak about my Shamanic practices, because the church isn't always accepting of such practices; it's more accepting of Islam, Judaism, Hinduism and Buddhism, the established faiths, than this.'

'While there are more people coming into church now that have porous boundaries between belief systems, that are moving between traditions, than say twenty years ago, I would still be careful about what I'd reveal.'

'And while I can't generalise and say that the church or the church authorities wouldn't accept Shamanism, there are people within the church who would think it is wonderful, and others who might see it as a disaster and regard me as a witch.'

Her journey into Shamanism began when Patricia tried to heal from the effects of childhood abuse inflicted upon her by a family member.

'My mother was a very disturbed woman, and I was a child lacking in love, so from age 7 to 22 this man offered me love but in an inappropriate way.'

'I was sexually abused by a member of the family, which I kept a secret through most of my childhood and a lot of my adulthood.'

Patricia's mental health suffered because of the abuse.

'I was ill, I was in a psychiatric hospital with mounds of pharmaceutical products, which I hated, and I felt I couldn't become who I really was'.

'I was desperate for a cure; it was obvious nobody was able to cure me and that psychiatry had nothing to offer and I went to a holistic medicine conference and met a neo-Shaman practitioner there. I made an appointment with her and asked her if she'd help me. And over four or five years, she did.'

'As well as being cured by the neo-Shaman, who also had a 1st class degree in medicine from Cambridge University, I learned from her.'

'Neo-Shamanism offered many things people would regard as superstitious, and psychiatry would say was rubbish, but I can say psychiatry was ineffective and this was healing.'

But Patricia didn't abandon her Christian faith in favour of her New Age learning, instead she combines them to serve her community.

'I would call myself a Christian priest using neo-Shamanic techniques.'

'We can't be Shamans because we've been brought up outside traditional Shamanic cultures, so we're neo-Shamans, we adapt the Shamanic practices within Western society'.

So how does Patricia reconcile the two guiding but potentially conflicting philosophies in her life?

'Shamanism is a belief system that wants people to fulfil their true vocation, nurturing people by means of various rituals, the power of love flowing through the universe. What the church would call God; Shamans would call simply love.'

'The Shamanic tradition has a view of an ensouled universe in which the trees, the plants, the stones, the bacteria need to work together.'

'The church would say you're on this planet once and then go to heaven, or maybe hell if you subscribe to that; but in Shamanism there's more of a belief in reincarnation – that you're reborn in some shape. It's also an inclusive belief system including the natural world as holy and sacred.'

'An awful lot of the stress in the church is on what you believe, not in what you do. So, while Christianity is a religion, Shamanism is less concerned with beliefs, but rather practices.'

'I'm more of a Christian minister, but I have Shamanic friends, and I will take people on journeys with the drum, I engage with what would be called the New Age communities. I'll create a ritual that I consider appropriate for that person and whatever it is they want to deal with.'

'There's a huge variation within the Christian religion; some people think Jesus should be worshipped as the Son of God, others that he should be imitated, rather than worshipped. There's a range of belief systems in the Christian church, with Orthodox and Roman Catholic at one end and Quakers at the other. There are many different versions of Christianity.'

'Witches, wizards are all part of the tradition of indigenous religion, tightly associated with the earth and containing degrees of what might be called magic or superstitions – all the things I was taught to despise at school. I'm not sure there's much difference between a spell that sends good energy to someone, and a prayer offered up in a Christian church. In the New Age you send them good energy, in Christian terms you pray for them. They may just be different words for describing the same thing.'

'I did a sound bath in the church recently, I took the singing bowls and the gongs and bells, people were lying on the floor and hearing the sounds. The New Age people were coming up and saying, 'I felt my throat chakra cleansed by it', the Christians came up and said, 'it's a wonderful way to pray.'

'As a Christian minister dealing with death and dying, I work with whatever belief system they have.'

'I share my Shamanic beliefs with people that I think will understand them, and not with those who wouldn't. I might also temper it by changing the language into one a Christian would recognise.'

'Belief is what Christianity has made of its religion, but I think spirituality is much more about what you do. Are you working from a base of love or something else?'

This is not to say Patricia does not also retain a strong and, in some ways, traditional Christian faith.

'I was always attracted to the ethos of the Church and the belief in the Trinity, and that God can be found in various contexts. Jesus showed us that God is not separate from humanity'.

'Jesus' life encouraged people to self-actualise, to be nurtured and to find out who they really are and who God intends them to be. It's a nurturing God that I support in my teaching.'

'There's also an element of service and serving and being concerned about other people, the poor, the asylum seekers, the prisoners, caring for people who may be uncared for or lost.'

'There are some bits of the Christian religion that are magnificent and other bits where we've twisted the story of Jesus.'

'I'm critical of the Christian use and encouragement of guilt.'

Patricia's vocation is to reach out and help those in need, her childhood abuse, her understanding of New Age practices and her strong faith, combine to make this possible.

'I'm good at listening to stories. My childhood abuse informs my work as a minister as I'm not shocked when I listen to people's stories, I'm a very good counsellor, I wouldn't be that if my childhood hadn't happened. It made me who I am and has given me a great deal of wisdom.'

This use of inner wisdom and insight drawn from many sources is also linked to Patricia's feminist studies and ideals.

'The Western world is very suspicious of intuition, it's traditionally a woman's art, which the patriarchy has systematically tried to destroy. It's something people keep secret because there's a negative association with much that is female and intuitive. What the patriarchy can't control it wants to eradicate.'

'The Christian religion became patriarchal once it became associated with the Roman Empire, which was a patriarchy. In the Roman Empire women only had two functions – privately to bear children and publicly to look ornamental. They had no other role.'

'But when I've studied Mary Magdalene, there was a strand of much more feminist, much more caring, much less rule-based Christianity. Mary Magdalene may have been an Egyptian goddess, or a priestess.'

'New Age thinking and neo-Shamanism has far more belief in goddesses and female power in the divine.'

'I see the great faiths as tarmacked roads, there are roundabouts where people are having interfaith dialogue, but at the sides of these roads there's a big woodland developing of a variety of practices, including Shamanic practices, mindfulness and transcendental meditation and all sorts of things. Possibly the new spiritual belief system is going to come from that woodland somewhere, rather than the church.'

'The woodland is where people who would call themselves spiritual rather than religious are situated, some of them are in groups, some are on their own.'

'What was last year's rebellion, becomes this year's orthodoxy. Look at the Beatles' popularisation of transcendental meditation in the 1960s; many people in the church thought it was an invention of the devil, but now it's more widely accepted.'

But she warns, 'anyone who claims to have absolute knowledge of the divine is dangerous, God is ultimately a mystery that we only know part of at any given time, enough to guide us.'

As she's grown older, Patricia worries less about talking about her practices.

'I'm too old not to say what I want. If I was young and had to make my way through the world, I would have to be much more careful, but in a sense, I have nothing to lose. I'm not looking to advance in my profession.'

'If I don't say what I want to now, I never shall say it. You might as well be hung for what you really are.'

'And if Christianity is about anything, it's about finding the kingdom of heaven within oneself; it's the recurring refrain from Jesus.'

'Maybe the church will get fed up with me and throw me out, but I will go on straddling the fields and bringing them together. In my experience an increasing number of people are interested in New Age stuff, it's a growing movement. I know at some point somebody may call me a witch, and that might cause me to be excommunicated.'

'But not being true to yourself is much worse than being persecuted from the outside.'

'I see myself as trying to reform the church from two centuries of patriarchy, to return to the messages from Jesus, and not messages from Jesus mangled by men for the last 2,000 years. As a minister I get a chance to speak to people for 10 or 15 minutes every Sunday.'

However, ultimately it was neo-Shamanism that has allowed Patricia to overcome her abuse and become who she is today. Patricia was failed by conventional responses to the mental health problems resulting from the abuse and her need to keep it secret.

'I took up Shamanism not because of the spirituality, but because of the disasters of 20th-century psychiatric medicine.'

'I was 7 when the abuse started and had grown up in a Christian family, so I felt like a miserable sinner because of the guilt induced by the church, and in a way the church played a role in me keeping the abuse secret.'

'If I had revealed the abuse, it would have broken up the family, and I certainly wasn't going to do that, even later.'

'Abuse went on to then happen in various contexts, including medical environments, so there's a whole history I have kept secret, which is why I was ill.'

'But the psychiatric profession couldn't handle that any more than the church could.'

'When I told a priest, they said I should tell so that he [the abuser] could be prosecuted, but I didn't want to, and so I was made to feel guilty again for not telling.'

The Christian faith has however offered Patricia a way of forgiving her abuser.

'The Christian faith says that Jesus was crucified, but he rose again, so that whatever has been done to you it can be redeemed. You can turn what's happened around into something beautiful.'

'That's where the Christian faith is useful, it says that there is nothing that a human being can do to another that can't be redeemed. It may take a long time, it may take a lot of work, but it can be done.'

'I wouldn't be the creative person I am today if it [the abuse] hadn't happened. Most of my achievements have come from that experience. It's caused me suffering but it's also a source of my creativity. There's a paradoxical view of it, I'm both grateful but it also made my life difficult and shouldn't have been done.'

'The Christian view of the crucifixion is that there is nothing that human beings can do in their viciousness and cruelty that can't, in the end, be turned around in some way; this is probably one of the things that holds me tight to Christianity.'

'For me the greatest mystery of the world is the mystery of suffering. For some people suffering can be turned around to creativity and for other people that doesn't appear to be true. Why?'

One of the reasons that Patricia doesn't speak about the abuse she suffered openly is because the man that abused her had a wife and children. After his death, with his children still alive, she retained the secret out of respect for them.

'I would tell my friends now, but when I mention him, his identity is well veiled.'

'His wife died before him, and he then invited me to see him again, but I didn't go.'

'The idea of forgiveness is interesting, the church says you must forgive more or less [by] tomorrow, but on the other hand you've got the therapeutic profession that says it's difficult and maybe even impossible to forgive. So, you've got two extremes.'

'It has taken a lot of work on my part, a lot of neo-Shamanic rituals and Christian rituals. There is hope, it's not the end of the world.'

So how has Patricia moved past her abuse?

'I waited until he died and then spent an hour talking with him in his coffin, telling him the results of what he'd done, and singing to him and telling him he was now free.'

'I saw him leave as a young man with Jesus, as a figure free from the guilt he'd experienced. Now most people would say it was an unconventional way of doing it, but I forgave him.'

'There are those I wouldn't talk to about the visionary experiences I've had, in the 20th century we've made the visionary experience madness, but increasingly people come to me with their visionary experiences.'

'I do see angels and I have seen them since I was a child. Shamanism has no problem with angels, and it was lovely going into neo-Shamanism from psychiatric medicine, which tends to see those things as not normal.'

'The limits of the church didn't serve me well [when it came to recovering from abuse], but Shamanism did.'

CHAPTER 15

ADHD and Mental Health

'As a teen, I started to get very angry about the fact I had ADHD because it was something that made me different to other people, so I kept it to myself. I didn't want anybody my own age to know, I barely wanted my teachers to know.'

Journalist **CJ DeBarra** was assigned female at birth but, now aged 40, identifies as non-binary. They were ten when they were diagnosed as having Attention Deficit Hyperactivity Disorder (ADHD) and Oppositional Defiant Disorder (ODD). At the time of diagnosis, they lived in rural West Cork and the concept of Special Educational Needs (SEN) support was non-existent. CJ's mother however knew she needed help with her child and visited several doctors to ensure CJ was correctly diagnosed.

ADHD is a lifespan neurodevelopmental condition that is thought to affect 1 in 5 people in the UK,[1] and it was first documented over 100 years ago. There are three traits of ADHD including hyperactivity, inattention and impulsivity, and anyone with a diagnosis of ADHD can be described as 'neurodiverse', meaning there is a difference in the way in which the brain functions.

ODD includes a frequent and ongoing pattern of anger, irritability, arguing and defiance toward parents and other authority figures. ODD also includes being spiteful and seeking revenge, categorised as vindictiveness.[2]

'My condition had an effect on everything from me doing my homework to my academic progression, to how I socialised, or rather didn't socialise, when I reached my teens.'

'At school I was inattentive, I was making mistakes, I was daydreaming, and I was also hyperactive, so I needed to be moving. I did really well in PE because it was a fantastic way of getting my energy out, but I found it really tough to sit still and do a lesson.'

Prior to being a teenager however, CJ admits being diagnosed as neurodivergent meant a great opportunity to miss school for various meetings with doctors and specialists. But that when their teenage hormones kicked in, they became very resentful.

'When I went to art college in 2004, I didn't tell anybody, I didn't tell my tutors or anyone in authority. It was a conscious decision because I felt it was something that marked me out as 'other' and, in my eyes, I was just as good as everybody else in the class and I was fed up with being told that I wasn't. I didn't want to be treated like I had learning difficulties, because I didn't.'

'A lot of the stuff we understand today, just wasn't around at that point. I remember being told in school that I wouldn't amount to anything, that I would never go anywhere.'

'I was raised as an Irish Catholic and taught by nuns. One told my mum I would never go to university and another, that there was nothing wrong with me, I just needed a good slap!'

'So yes, when I moved away from school and went to university, with experiences like that, I didn't tell anyone, I wanted to be treated the same as my peers, and because I'd been told I'd never achieve anything I wanted to show them otherwise, it acted as a massive kick up the backside and I went and did a Masters in Journalism,' says CJ.

'I've lost jobs as a result of having ADHD and not disclosing it, because employers have wondered why I've made inattentive mistakes, why I've daydreamed in meetings, why I've been glued to my phone in place of a stimming toy.'

'In 2013 I started a PhD in politics, and that was the first time I told any organisation or workplace that I had ADHD since being diagnosed in 1996, until then I'd kept that information to myself.'

Growing up, CJ struggled to find anyone like themselves, despite current research suggesting that one out of seven people will be neurodivergent in some way.[3] It seems they were not the only one keeping quiet.

'In Ireland we do a really good job of looking the other way when it comes to mental health and we really don't talk about it. We don't talk about a lot of stuff, and I don't know why. I think it's probably a hangover from the days when we were much more under the rule of the Catholic church, but I think culturally too, there's a thing about not admitting when you're feeling bad.'

'When I moved to secondary school and my class size was much bigger than at primary, you just didn't talk about it. It was an embarrassment in a way, the last thing you want to do age 13 is to be any different from your class, you're dying to fit in, so if you had ADHD or dyslexia or anything that made you different, you didn't talk about it.'

'I didn't knowingly meet another ADHD person that wasn't male until I was maybe 32, and as I was raised as a female, it was a long time to go not seeing anyone like yourself. I was so shocked when she told me she had ADHD, I didn't know what to say.'

But having ADHD also meant CJ was less likely to fulfil the gendered expectation of rural West Ireland in the 1990s, which was that while many boys returned to their family farm to work after school, the girls would become teachers. Not only did their diagnosis mean that gaining a degree in an academic subject would be harder, their neurodivergent trait of being unable to tolerate loud noises, ruled out a career with children. This opened the opportunity of art college for them.

But CJ regrets staying silent for so long.

'I wish I'd spoken about it sooner, because I didn't properly understand things like the social model of disability. I didn't understand I was facing barriers that I shouldn't have been and that my classmates didn't have, but I was still expecting to be able to produce the same level of work at the same quality. It wasn't that I wasn't capable, it was that society was throwing up different barriers. If I had spoken up about what I was facing, things could have been put in place.'

However, it is often not enough to speak up, you also have to educate yourself about what you need, to be able to ensure the correct support structures are put in place.

'When I finally did speak to my university about my ADHD, it put stuff in place, but it was things like extra time in exams and the use of a laptop. But I didn't know much about neurodiversity at that point, and I didn't need those things, I needed something else. I'd been denying the fact I had ADHD for so long, so I didn't bother to learn anything about it, I didn't bother to engage with it. Had I done that, I could have learnt so much more about my brain and how it works.'

'Now I realise that had I understood myself more I could have asked for things like a stimming toy in an office environment or known to have asked permission to use headphones in an open plan setting. I didn't know how much those things could benefit me.'

'This lack of knowledge affected the grades I got, it meant I dropped out of my PhD because I struggled with things like finding and filling in the right funding forms. I ended up burning out because I was working nearly full-time hours around a part-time PhD. Today I think we would be better educated, and someone could go to an access support worker and explain they were having difficulty with something and ask for help.'

Looking back at missed opportunities and lost jobs, CJ says:

'I wish I'd been honest and open about the fact that my brain works differently. I was brought up with the medical model of disability that places the emphasis on the impairment and that the impairment has been a barrier. I just felt I had something wrong with me.'

'I worried if I told an employer in an interview, they might not hire me, because they're going to have to spend the whole time looking after me.'

'But in reality, the adjustments I need are very small, nothing expensive or time consuming, just little tweaks here and there that help me to stay in the workplace.'

But for CJ it wasn't just their professional life that was affected by not talking about their neurodiversity.

'I wondered so much about the effects of keeping my neurodivergence a secret in relationships, and sex and love, that I wrote a whole book about it from a queer, neurodivergent perspective. I would disclose my ADHD on occasion but in a jokey way to pass it off. I didn't spend any time explaining to partners that I was neurodivergent, that I had ADHD, and this is what I need. That only begun to happen after I wrote the book in 2023.'

'After I wrote the book I came out as neurodivergent in my personal life and in my workplace as well, and I'm now asking for my access needs to be met, applying for things like Personal Independence Payment (PIP) and rail cards, and putting things in place to help myself.'

What advice does CJ have for others in the same boat as them, wondering if they are ready to talk about their neurodivergence and how they should do so?

'Disclosure is a very personal thing. It's going to be different for everybody. When I get asked when the right time is to tell somebody about your neurodivergence, the honest answer is it's going to be different for everybody. But you've got to be ready, and you've got to work out what the benefits are for you in disclosing, and whether you feel safe to do that.'

'If you're going to disclose, know what your condition looks like for you. What are your traits? If you know what your traits are, you can start looking at what your needs are, like headphones or quiet spaces at work, or in a relationship explaining that you struggle with arguments or can't process emotions very quickly. Be proactive and lay the groundwork.'

'And it's not up to you to have all the answers immediately. Also, your needs will change over time. I thought I had all the answers to my ADHD and then perimenopause came along. I had to completely reassess what I did, what I needed, how that impacted my traits.'

'The hormones connected to perimenopause can change everything, just at a time when you are confident in what you can and can't cope with, who you feel comfortable with. For me it's affected how I travel. I can't drive because of my ADHD, so I use public transport, but my balance has been affected so I need to be helped off trains, I need passenger support to meet me and help me on and off. Things like the patterns of tiles or high ceilings can disorient me and cause a fall, so I go into shutdown and can't move.'

CJ stresses though that the most important thing is to always be comfortable with talking to others about your neurodivergence.

'I've disclosed in the past and it hasn't always been on my terms, but I think the lay of the land is different now, neurodiversity is more accepted, people are more educated about it.'

The days of hiding their neurodivergence and suffering because of that are now behind them.

Worries over Neurodiverse Acceptance

'I sought out my ADHD diagnosis in 2022 to turn the stigma around neurodiverse labels on their head a bit. I'd read some great articles about brilliant women with ADHD and in a moment of clarity I decided I needed to understand my own traits better.'

Jenny is 43, and her eldest child, who is now 11, was diagnosed as being on the autistic spectrum when he was three and she says, at the time, the general feeling was not to put a label on neurodiverse children, as if it was something to be ashamed or scared of.

'It changed my life as a mother having my son's diagnosis, but I was determined to see past the stigma of the label of being autistic. I'm the trustee of a charity and so it's up to me to advocate for the community.'

'A few years ago, I was having certain struggles in my own life, and I'd seen how official diagnoses had helped other ADHD ambitious women but also that the shame of that had affected them. But I wanted to understand how having different neural pathways could be a brilliant thing.'

Covering up the way her brain worked was beginning to drain Jenny of all the energy required to be a working mum of three.

'I was jumping from one thing to another, looking for the dopamine hits I'd had when I was younger, when I was the fun, chaotic, impulsive type. I was drinking and trying to keep a lid on all the chaos in my brain and be the perfect mother. But I was finding it harder and harder to bring any control into my life and as you get older, and when you have people relying on you, it's no longer acceptable to live in chaos. Then the shame was kicking in, I felt like life was supposed to be in some kind of better order and I was failing at that.'

'Looking after my kids to the right level was a worthwhile sacrifice, but it took everything in my power to do it.'

To help herself cope, Jenny had wisely created her own support system.

'I learnt to use a lot of physical visuals, like calendars, books and lists, to keep on top of everything. I know I need to be hypervigilant when my son starts secondary school later this year so that I can keep his school life in order.'

But despite her positive outlook on what being neurodiverse can offer, Jenny is still reluctant to tell many people about her own diagnosis.

'My mother suffers from a lot of mental health issues; it wouldn't do her any favours if I told her. Telling people is about weighing up the value it would have both to me and the other person.'

'I've told my husband, although sometimes I wish I hadn't as it hasn't made me feel much better. He tries to understand but he's just very different to me.'

'But I've also told my two closest friends who have been brilliant. If I'm being hard on myself, I'll call them because I know they look at me through rose-tinted glasses and will be kind.'

'I do feel shame that I've not told people in my workplace at all, particularly as I'm a representative of an autism charity where we try to ditch that shame and be open.'

And it's within her professional life that Jenny worries that being open about her ADHD could have the most effect.

'I feel so lucky to work in the media, and I don't want to do anything that would put that at risk. But I also think that there are so many female journalists coming out as ADHD now that I might even be thought of as jumping on the bandwagon. There's an ennui about it.'

'I'm worried about how being open about ADHD could affect my prospects, because of the perceptions people have of those with a diagnosis. It could be seen as a huge inconvenience to an employer, at a newspaper for example, where part of the job involves staying on top of lots of stories all at the same time. I can juggle projects, but I do need to use apps and lists to help me stay organised, and I've become adept at that.'

'I've also had a lot of experience of live TV, which I loved and was successful at, but I'd be exhausted afterwards. Although I'm drawn to the jeopardy of roles like that!'

And it's not only work where Jenny might hear negative viewpoints about neurodiversity.

'In social circles people can be very opinionated, they don't hold back. I think because my son is autistic, that might soften people's viewpoints a bit, but I know some of them feel that labels are bandied around willy nilly, particularly those close to education. They might think people use it as an excuse or that it's become cool and trendy to claim to be neurodiverse.'

'I find that mortifying and worry that will be the next damaging opinion for the community, especially women who do mask more. This attitude will stop them from coming out and seeking a diagnosis.'

'I find that sad because as a society we'd moved past the fear of labels and were embracing it for a while, but now it feels like opinion is turning again.'

'But I guarantee no woman is saying they are neurodiverse because they want to be cool.'

To some extent, Jenny is also still coming to terms with the implications of her diagnosis and what the future might hold as she approaches perimenopause.

'There is a real period of mourning, realising I can't carry on the way I did now that I have the responsibilities that I do. I have a horrible fear I'm going to go hard into menopause and experience a rollercoaster of highs and lows. I watched the Chris Packham documentary and the effect of a lack of oestrogen on ADHD was covered there. It can send the ADHD brain into further chaos.'

'I also feel bad about not telling my children about my diagnosis, and I don't really know why. I don't want them to feel unsafe having an ADHD mum or worry that I'm not going to pick them up at the right time or forget something important. But I do hold my hands up to them and say I sometimes do things differently to other mums, but we get there, we're all good.'

But being neurodiverse also makes Jenny a better parent, being understanding of what her children might be feeling. One of Jenny's ADHD traits is that she can be very clumsy, but she's keen that her children never feel that you can't make mistakes.

'If someone knocks something over, I'll always say we all make mistakes, and I want them to know that we can't be perfect.'

One thing that might convince Jenny to be more open is if her children ever need her to be.

'If one of my younger children needed any kind of support with an issue like this, then it would be relevant for me to talk more about my diagnosis to help them, that would be my only driver to be more open.'

People will Judge

Personal Trainer **Emma McCaffrey** is 47 and lives in Hampshire. She runs Move With Emma, a business that focusses on women and how physical movement can support the mind. For Emma this comes from a lifelong experience of dealing with the shame often associated with mental illness. Three years ago, Emma was diagnosed with ADHD but will only tell people about her neurodiversity and mental health if she knows they won't judge.

'I'm getting to a point where I really don't talk about ADHD because I don't feel it should define me, because people make judgements, just like they do with mental illness.'

'I'm also from a generation where it's ingrained in me, that once the cat's out of the bag, that's it.'

When it comes to talking about her mental health, Emma feels similarly judged as she suffers from depression.

Depression (also called major depressive disorder or clinical depression) can cause severe symptoms that affect how you feel, think, and handle daily activities, such as sleeping, eating, or working.[4] Research shows one in six adults in the UK experiences a common mental health problem, such as depression or anxiety, and that women are more likely (19%) than men (14%) to report experiencing some form of depression.[5]

'I feel shame and guilt too, because of the narrative of what have I got to be depressed about? I'm privileged, I have a roof over my head, a family that love me, I had a middle-class upbringing.'

'There's a whole misunderstanding about what depression is, as if it's a choice. People think you can snap out of it. I fear that I seem ungrateful, that I don't have the right to this illness because I'm not struggling, that I've got nothing to be sad about.'

Emma's recent ADHD diagnosed has helped her understand more about herself and the way she approaches life, and why that can sometimes be more difficult than it should be.

'For years I was diagnosed with generalised anxiety disorder, but now we realise that for women with ADHD it's a hyperactivity in your brain, overthinking, getting into loops, spiralling. I get fixated and stuck on something but in contrast to that I'm also impulsive, spontaneous, brave and can handle lots. I'm good in a crisis, I used to work on live TV, so I'm in my element dealing with fast moving things. But if I get burned out, I can get overwhelmed by the smallest thing; even getting out of bed, or leaving the house, can be a mountain to climb.'

Growing up, Emma had a mixed response when she asked for help and support. It was perhaps a sign of the times.

'My dad was supportive when I was taking medication, although my mum is more anti-medication generally, and for anything, even a headache (and more focused on non-medicalised solutions). When I was a lot younger though, mental illness was just really misunderstood. I used to cry a lot, and I couldn't snap out of it. I didn't understand it, and I was scared. There were some people I could talk to and that's a massive relief, but I've slowly moved away from people who have a negative view about mental illness, particularly if I've recently had an episode, as that can make me feel really uncomfortable and unsafe.'

'It's the same with the ADHD diagnosis, it's said to be becoming a trend and people say it's being over-diagnosed. And I do think some people go for a diagnosis, particularly with kids, because the way our schooling system is set up, you have to have the label to get the allowances, adaptations and access to resources they perhaps need. It seems like a bit of a vicious circle.'

Deep down however, despite the social programming that might make Emma feel she should hide both her ADHD diagnosis and her struggle with depression, she knows that being neurodiverse does not mean you cannot thrive in the right environment.

'What we need is society to accept that there are lots of different types of brains, it's been set up to suit neurotypical brains and that's a narrow subset, but it's about getting the right environment, the right role for the right brain. People with ADHD can be creative, and most entrepreneurs have ADHD, so if you find the right environment, the right type of pressure, you can really thrive with ADHD.'

'I came out of the education system thinking I was not enough because I didn't fit into their very narrow criteria of what success looks like. You can feel like a failure, and it stunts people's ability to flourish and fulfil their potential because it affects confidence.'

'But the current system was set up in response to the industrial revolution, it was all about the production line. Now that's obsolete, but I think it'll be a long time before we get to a society that sees people as types, with each type of brain offering benefits, talent and something beneficial to contribute.'

'But with the increasing gig-style working world it's really helpful to have people who can think and approach things in different ways.'

Emma sought out an official diagnosis for the way in which her brain works, not because she needed more information for herself, although it did have a pleasant side effect of deeper self-awareness, but because she recognised her daughter was also experiencing some difficulties.

'The reason I got diagnosed was that my eldest daughter was having a lot of problems at school and struggling, and I was trying to figure it out. And this was four years ago, before there was a lot of information about how ADHD looks different in girls and that it's been under diagnosed in females.'

'She was getting overwhelmed and paralysed and not being able to do anything, so I was looking up, trying to understand it, and I thought 'my god I've got ADHD.'

From her research, Emma was able to understand herself and both her daughters better and put in place some coping mechanisms.

'I think my eldest daughter has Attention Deficit Disorder (ADD), because she doesn't have the hyperactivity, but she's got the distraction element. My younger one I think has ADHD. But I'm not having them diagnosed because they are high functioning and thriving, and while I think a diagnosis is good for self-awareness, I don't really use my diagnosis.'

'That's what I'm trying to instil in them. My youngest has fidget toys, as she struggles to sit still, she's really clumsy but she is doing well at school. Recently she said to her teacher at the end of a lesson where they had noticed she was getting chatty and distracted that she was struggling to sit still because she has ADHD and they congratulated her that she was aware of it. Which is wonderful.'

'I want to empower them that if they find themselves in the situations, I've found myself in, that they've got the language to cope and that they don't see their inability to cope in certain environments or situations as a sign of their failure. I don't want them to get backed into a corner and feel that they are different and not as good.'

'The approach has worked with my eldest who was stressed and school refusing, so I went with my instinct and allowed her to stay away from school for a short period. Instead, she came and helped at my outdoor classes managing the music and motivating middle-life women, and then she spent some time with her dad, and then she came to me and said she was ready to go back to school.'

'I've tried to give her some power because school is obedience and compliance-focussed. I don't want to create problems, and I don't want her to feel over-indulged. Working with her dad, and a great teacher she has, we've built up her confidence. Now she's got the lead role in the school play, spoken at the church service, she's confident and she's comfortable in her own skin and most importantly she is content and enjoying life.'

'Both my girls are learning to be aware of their characters and emotions, and I'm only just learning things like this about myself at 47!'

In the past, Emma often didn't understand why she was struggling and blamed herself. She shied away from talking about how she felt, scared it made her different and a failure. She didn't want to acknowledge her mental illness, hoping perhaps that it would somehow go away by itself.

'I'm cautious about labels and getting put in a box or pathologizing traits that may be my personality, but after my own diagnosis it was like a lightbulb moment. Now I understand why I've suffered. I think my first bout of depression was at age 14, it can be cyclical or in response to life events, but when I found out about ADHD, I realised that's part of the reason why I've suffered from anxiety and depression and

I had felt so weak and ashamed, like I had failed. I had this thing and I felt it was my inability to control it that was the problem.'

'I thought I must be weak and useless, a freak show, I didn't see it was because of society, and I was scared of it too. When I got poorly, I had to deal with trying to recover as well as being in denial. I'd resist, but each time I'd have to go to therapy. I have to take medication, and it's exhausting, its expensive. It's like your whole life feels black, and the things that bring you joy aren't there anymore.'

'When I'm not poorly I don't want to think about it, I don't want to talk about it because if I do, it's almost like I'm willing myself back there, I just pretend I'm not going to get it again.'

'With depression they say if you've had it more than three times then it's always waiting in the wings/likely to come back. Every day I feel like I'm swimming against the tide, just to be myself and to stay afloat. I'm such a happy person and laid back, which is a contradiction, I know.'

'I can feel wobbly, because I have past experiences that make me scared, and I never want to go back there because it's like you're being pulled under by something that's out of your control, into a big black hole, and then you know you're going to be gone for three or six months, and it's horrible because you are missing out on life, and I love life. I love little things like having a cup of tea, and I'm so frightened of that, despite feeling very well at the moment.'

Not knowing about her neurodiversity, along with a lack of public knowledge about ADHD, and not wanting to talk about how her mental health was suffering often because of it, has meant that relationships can be harder for Emma.

'ADHD does impact your relationships because of emotional dysregulation; I get overwhelmed and heightened.'

'A boyfriend sent me an article that described ADHD as being the latest trend, suggesting it's a label, it's a tool to organise people and something to piggyback on and become lazier, to claim benefits. I took that badly, I felt unsupported and like he was saying I was taking on an identity.'

'But I'm not that person, I'm doing it for self-awareness to help myself. I used to think if I couldn't do a spreadsheet or deal with numbers then I was a failure, and so stupid. But with the diagnosis I know it's just more challenging because of the way my brain works. It's not my fault, I'm not lazy. Now I can sit myself down and say, I find this difficult, how can I overcome it? The diagnosis is a breakthrough for me, and I'm processing it.'

'But you also feel angry, because you don't want to have this and things are harder for me. The energy it takes when my mind is going around and around, it's so tiring. And then you've got this strong inner critic and this energy too. It causes burnout as you believe you can do everything and don't notice when you reach your limits or until it's too late.'

'My ex-husband did understand; he told me that I would have to manage my mental health just as a recovering addict would. He said I would always have it, and it is something I need to be aware of and manage and that I needed to have things in place to prevent a relapse. It was a little shocking as I had never thought about it in that way. His advice came from a place of love.'

'I've also discussed my ADHD diagnosis with him, because it impacts our children. And my ADHD traits did affect our marriage. I could get anxious and disengaged, which would make it seem that I didn't care. On the flipside, dysregulation, fear and anxiety can result in getting overwhelmed and overstimulated resulting in me becoming reactive.'

But why do women keep mental illness and neurodiversity secret, and do they do that more than men?

Emma says, 'I think women are expected to show up and be happy, which is why so many women with ADHD and mental health problems mask so well. Because of this demand there's an added shame and fear for a woman of being labelled, and looking like you haven't got it together, or you're not good or being nice.'

'ADHD was so misunderstood, women were ashamed, and we don't want to reveal the traits, we don't want to stand out, we don't want to drop a ball. In the 90s when we were stepping into masculine energy in the workplace, for example, we didn't want to show any signs of weakness. Look at the criticism Chancellor of the Exchequer Rachel Reeves got recently when she cried in Parliament, it was front page news.'

'But crying is normal, and if people around you struggle to accept it or think it means you're having a complete breakdown, it can make you feel you're in the wrong.'

'Women have had to work harder to be accepted in the workplace. If you wanted to be promoted to a senior role, you couldn't be seen to have emotions, and while we're beginning to understand that feminine traits are powerful and things are changing, for a time feminism was masking the fact we were doing it all, entering the workplace but still doing it all at home too.'

'Women are often expected to have an amazing career but also be an excellent mother, and women are burning out because of all of the demands on them.'

'And hormones massively affect our mental wellbeing, during pregnancy and afterwards, and then menopause. It can be relentless being a woman.'

'And even with the better understanding we have of menopause now, it's still in danger of making women out to be lesser, that we can't cope. But it makes us more resilient because we're dealing with this as well as life.'

Certain sections of the media have also discouraged Emma from discussing the issues.

'I think we hide mental health challenges and neurodiversity because of the negative connotations from the right-wing media. It can make you feel scared and vulnerable, that people will think you're jumping on a bandwagon, like I'm making myself a victim. But that's a hideous idea, because this has had such an impact on my life, and what would I have to gain from doing that?'

'I think the over-diagnosis is diminishing people's struggle, but it's always people that haven't experienced it that are commenting negatively. It's easy for them to say that people are begging for funds, allowances and grants.'

'I've read some scathing pieces on ADHD, and that makes it harder to be open about my diagnosis, to put myself out there because it makes me feel uncomfortable and reinforces all the reasons that I've concealed it in the past.'

But Emma remains keen to break the taboos around mental health and neurodiversity, opening up here, and to those she trusts, and to those she might also offer knowledgeable support to, like those she teaches. But there remains an element of reticence.

'I want to help other people by being relatable. I want to be open, but I do wonder at what cost to me and what benefit it would have for others?'

References

1. https://www.adhdfoundation.org.uk/resources/what-is-adhd (accessed Sept 2025)
2. https://www.mayoclinic.org/diseases-conditions/oppositional-defiant-disorder/symptoms-causes/syc-20375831 (accessed Sept 2025)
3. https://www.local.gov.uk/lga-libdem-group/our-press-releases/neurodiversity#:~:text=What%20is%20neurodiversity?,learns%20and%20processes%20information%20differently. (accessed Sept 2025)
4. https://www.nimh.nih.gov/health/topics/depression (accessed Sept 2025)
5. https://www.priorygroup.com/mental-health/depression-treatment/depression-statistics (accessed Sept 2025)

CHAPTER 16

Weight-loss Jabs

'The world is too judgey for me, and I think part of not sharing is looking after my mental health. There's nothing worse than being told you are a failure at something, or that you're not doing it right'.

Joanna, 55, a psychiatric nurse in the Southwest of England, has been taking weight-loss jabs for the last six months. In that time, she's lost a stone. But the only person that knows her secret is her husband, who supports her decision.

Weight-loss injections like Mounjaro (tirzepatide) and Wegovy (semaglutide) are GLP-1 agonists and mimic a hormone your body releases after eating called GLP-1 (glucagon-like peptide-1). The drugs trigger the release of the hormone called insulin into the bloodstream, which lowers blood sugar levels. GLP-1 also slows down digestion, lowering appetite and makes those taking it feel fuller after eating. People taking the drug feel less hungry, eat less, and lose weight.

Like many women, Joanna's history with body image and weight loss is complicated. As a teenager she modelled but was considered plus size as she wore a size 14 in clothes. With a muscular frame, she was also sporty and a successful long-distance runner and javelin thrower. Her mother had also modelled in her youth, and was a former beauty queen, but both her parents thought that women bore a responsibility to look a certain way to attract and keep their man. Subsequently, her mother went on to have an eating disorder.

'During my sporting background my weight was measured and controlled too.'

'I do think the judgement about size is worse if you're a woman. You only have to look at clothes – men's sports clothes come in triple X size, and they are often loose, not Lycra, clinging to every bit of fat on your body. But I do think men are becoming more body conscious, we've continued to judge women, and the same judgement is moving into the manosphere. We've gone in the wrong direction and found a new group to intimidate as well!'

Joanna has some past experience with trying to lose weight.

'I battled with my weight after I had my son at 18, and I have gone to slimming clubs like Slimming World. But I always kept it quiet, and I don't think it mattered so much that I kept something like this secret in the 80s or 90s. But now, social media encourages people to share everything.'

'While years ago, I might have sat and chatted with my friends and discussed trying to lose weight, shaming experiences at those weight-loss clubs have made me uncomfortable with feeling judged. I would feel like I had done something wrong if I'd not lost weight each week, despite the changes sometimes being hormonal, and I'd also feel judged if I was enjoying a meal out and was overweight.'

'But sitting with a few friends and chatting is very different to sharing it on the social networks we have today, which have become so big. I could be sharing it with 500 people and not just six girlfriends.'

Taking the jabs was not a quick decision for Joanna, not least because of her own experience as a nurse.

'The medical profession can also be quite judgmental. There are a lot of assumptions that you're overweight because you are eating too much, and have takeaways every night, that you eat junk food, sweets and cake.'

'Because of my nursing background, and because I've worked

in eating disorder units, I wondered if I really wanted to take the weight-loss jabs. I spoke to a GP about my weight however and got nowhere, not even a referral for a dietician. Ironically, because I'd lost a stone and a half by myself, I wasn't fat enough to qualify for help.'

'I also have Chronic Fatigue Syndrome (CFS) which reduces my activity levels, exercise is not advised, and it makes symptoms worse. But if you tell people that, they think it's just an excuse.'

Joanna also feels her nursing career means she is subject to extra judgement from sceptics.

When Joanna decided to take the jabs, she knew she was keen not to follow the example set by many online influencers and reality TV celebrities, who seem to lose weight very quickly by upping their doses to the maximum as soon as possible.

'I thought to myself, I'm going to do it my way and lose weight slowly. I had a friend who did the jabs but very quickly went up to the highest dose. She ended up having palpitations and many of the side effects.'

'I used to belong to a Facebook group that talked about the injection, but I left as I felt a lot of the posts weren't healthy for me to read. People would say they had lost three stone after two months on the jab. My nurse side would come out then too.'

Joanna also says she hasn't shared the details of her decision to use weight-loss jabs because of the fear of failure.

'If you don't succeed on these jabs, you open yourself up to everyone offering you advice you don't want, but I want to ask them where's the scientific evidence for what they are saying. There's so much information out there on the Internet, but it's not always evidence based, and it's not always true.

'I also don't want to be bothered about getting into arguments with people about my decision to take the jabs, asking if I've done this or that. With CFS I don't have the spare emotional energy and time for that, I can't be bothered with the negativity.'

'People will talk about losing weight by taking more exercise, but I've trained for eight months to run a marathon and stayed the same size. For health indicators I look at heart rate, blood pressure and lung capacity, I'd rather that went down.'

Protecting a Professional Reputation

'It's been comical at times, with me lurking outside the front door of my flat, for hours on end, once a month, to intercept the delivery driver with my next package of the drug. Just to avoid the risk of someone else in my building finding out,' says **Margaret**, a barrister in her early 60s.

At just 17, Margaret headed off to Cambridge University to read law and today practises in the field of personal injury and clinical negligence. For the last 26 weeks however she has been a secret Mounjaro user and has not told a soul. In that time, she has lost five stone, and people are noticing.

'I continue to lie and say my weight loss is purely down to a mix of willpower and lifestyle changes.'

Margaret says that there's a variety of reasons she keeps her use of weight-loss jabs a secret.

'The first is embarrassment that I needed the drug to finally conquer my life-long weight problem. I don't lack self-discipline or will power so why has my weight been my Achilles heel?'

Allied with this embarrassment, Margaret also admits her motivation for wanting to lose weight isn't just her health.

'If I am honest, I see this drug as my last shot at regaining some attractiveness. I am divorced and after years of caring for my parents and my son, I am alone and free to pursue what I alone want.'

But this desire to be physically appealing despite her age brings up some ideological contradictions for Margaret.

'In my case I feel embarrassed partly because being a child of the 1960s, I am a feminist and so I think I shouldn't care if my hair is grey and I'm fat. And yet I do! I wonder if there's an element of somehow trying to justify why I was overweight, trying to bluster that I didn't care, when I very much did. My son and my friends have been extremely encouraging for me to get out and date again, so I think my mindset was the problem, not a wider societal issue.'

Margaret's chosen profession is the second reason she keeps her use of weight-loss jabs under wraps. She orders her drugs from online supplier Juniper, which offers the Mounjaro drug, and has 150,000 members on its site.

'I was invited by Juniper to become the face of the drug and to tell my story, but I declined because I didn't want to be accused of bringing my profession into disrepute. The Bar is very unforgiving of such things,' she says.

'As a profession the law is restrictive, more so than many. The Bar Council and Law Society both have codes of conduct. The Bar's code runs to 106 pages, and exhorts us to act with honesty, independence and integrity in all aspects of our professional and personal lives. I had to report to the Bar Council that I had a speeding fine two years ago! I'm not saying taking a weight-loss drug in secret is a breach of the code, but if my name or image were associated commercially with Juniper then I think that would raise eyebrows. I don't want to take that risk.'

The upside of her profession however is that she has plenty of experience in keeping quiet.

'I don't find it hard to keep a secret. I think that is mainly down to 36 years of legal practice though, where confidentiality is drummed into us!'

Margaret's third reason for secrecy is judgement.

'I do not want to be associated in some way with the overwhelmingly negative perception of this drug in the mainstream media, in particular the ghastly *Daily Mail*-type readership.'

'Media coverage of weight-loss drugs is very high, with stories daily. Only today there was an alarmist item in *The Guardian* regarding pancreatitis. Looking at the figures, there are fewer than 300 cases of it, and no real analysis of whether the victims had pre-existing issues. *The Daily Mail* has virtually a daily negative item showcasing some weight-loss user speaking of regrets and the 'terrible' side effects. By contrast there are hardly any positive stories of those who have lost many kilos and feel they have been given their lives back. Reading the Juniper community page on Facebook is wonderfully affirming, to see just how many users, like me, are utterly delighted and wish only that they had started sooner.'

Margaret believes there is a certain stigma attached to using the drugs.

'It's openly painted by some people as 'cheating' somehow, but this stems from a fundamental misunderstanding, the drugs don't cause weight loss in themselves but facilitate it by stopping hunger from being felt. The user still has to maintain a strict calorie deficit and make significant changes to their lifestyle. Taking the drug alone without the rest of the work will have no effect.'

'I also think there is a degree of envy by some, because the drugs are expensive, well over £200 a month.'

And the price only looks set to rise, with headlines suggesting the cost of GLP-1 will spike by 170 per cent from September 2025.

Margaret also thinks the stigma attached to taking weight-loss jabs is because of a lack of understanding about what creates obesity.

'Being overweight is not just because we are lazy and eat rubbish. For many, it's the deafening, constant 'food noise', the finishing of one meal and then immediately thinking about the next, the drug miraculously turns this off.'

But is the judgement worse for women, causing more of us to keep its use quiet?

'It is worse for women, and I find usually the criticism is from other women. This is something I never understand. It's tough enough being a woman in any aspect of life, without those who should be our natural allies not providing support. Just watch *Loose Women* to see what I mean.'

'In my experience, men definitely do not feel the same pressure to keep this sort of thing private. My colleagues and friends of the male persuasion are far simpler creatures in every way!'

But Margaret does not feel that her family and friends would be judgemental if she were to tell them about her use of the jabs.

'None of this explains why I have kept it quiet from my friends and family, in particular my son who is 27 and a teacher. He is deeply loving and supportive of me in every way. I know he would not judge me. I keep this from him because I want to be selfish! The journey is mine and mine alone.'

For Maragret there is a level of enjoyment of keeping her secret, although she's not entirely under cover.

'I get a certain frisson in keeping this quiet!'

'But I was still happy to reach out for this book, and I post virtually daily on the Juniper community page, so part of me clearly wants to share!'

Of course, keeping secrets can lead to misunderstandings and assumptions, and Margaret suspects this has happened in the workplace.

'One area where this has been funny is at work. Colleagues are now openly commenting and being very sweet about my obvious weight loss. For a while though I could see them wanting to say something but being fearful that perhaps I was ill. So, my poor assistant found herself fielding questions about my health!'

Telling Someone Doesn't Mean They'd Understand

'I'm lying to these people, but I don't want to go through that conversation about whether I'm doing it the right or wrong way.'

The conversation that **Louise**, who is 51 and an Australian living in Scotland, is referring to is one that will be familiar to anyone taking weight-loss jabs. Whether or not using them is 'cheating'.

'People can be so judgemental. People say to me 'at least you're losing weight in the right way', referring to the fact I've become more active and am eating healthy food. And I am doing that, but I'm not open about the support I'm getting from the medication, which enables me to that.'

'It just frees my brain to be able to do the things I've always wanted to do, which is make healthy choices without a fight about it in my head.'

For Louise explaining the complex relationship she and many others have with diet and exercise is difficult and often falls on deaf ears.

'There's a lot of misunderstanding about what the drug does. I'm coming up to my one-year anniversary in a few weeks' time. What it's done for me is cleared my brain so that the whole food noise has gone, so what I've always wanted to do about making healthy choices is possible. It's always been a huge battle for me; my whole day would be a complete struggle.'

'Before the jabs, losing weight was a struggle. I have this unusual response to being full that only affects about three per cent of the population: I sneeze. But it still didn't stop me from eating, even though if I was sneezing, I knew I was full, my brain knew I was full, but eating was an obsession I'd battled with my whole life.'

When Louise started using weight-loss jabs she weighed 23 stone, and she's since lost 10 stone. As she lives alone, it's been easy to access the medication without the need to hide it. But she has confided in those she feels safe with.

'About two months ago I told two very close friends. It was because on a night out a conversation started about a person using the drug when they were very slightly overweight, and people using the drugs because they were diabetic and prediabetic. The discussion was very much about the right and wrong uses.'

'I didn't say anything then, but I reflected on it and later sent a detailed message to the WhatsApp group we share. After reading it, both friends were very supportive because they can see the difference it has made for me.'

But Louise still feels that it's a struggle for people to understand the impact the weight loss has on your mental health.

'Exercise releases endorphins, but when you're very heavy, any movement causes pain and so you avoid it.'

'I was also avoiding social situations. I got anxious about them because of my size and people looking at me and judging me physically, and also how I could deal with moving about. I couldn't walk far or up a hill, so I'd have to worry what the evening out meant in physical terms. I avoided seeing people and doing things, and I just felt really uncomfortable in my life.'

'Eventually it was a work event that made my mind up about taking the jabs. It was a global, team building thing, a citywide treasure hunt. And I just knew I couldn't walk about for the two hours. I was always at the back of the pack, with a few compassionate people keeping me company. But I was embarrassed and felt guilty. I felt humiliated and I thought I just can't do this anymore. That's when I started on the medication.'

'Now I walk everywhere I go. I see a personal trainer once a week for weight training, I do aquafit twice a week, and I do Pilates. I feel fully engaged in my life again.'

With all this positive improvement, both physical and mental, would Louise be happy to share her use of the drug with more people eventually?

'I do feel I want to share the positives of weight-loss jabs, but I don't know if I'd ever be ready to do so because my concern is that the more people know, the more likely it is that people wouldn't have a conversation with me about it but simply talk behind my back. And I'd also have to apologise for not telling them previously.'

After leaving her last position, which required a lot of travelling and was in part to blame for Louise often eating takeaways due to the exhaustion and time restrictions of flying, Louise recently enjoyed several months gardening leave at her parents' house back in Australia. But she didn't share her use of the jab with her parents.

'It was a bit tougher for me to hide it, but my mum would have freaked out because she would have worried about the side effects. She's in her mid-70s, so I didn't want to put her through that. I had to find a spot in the back of the fridge to hide it and find a place to inject myself in secret.'

While Louise's mother isn't anti-medication, taking several pills daily for ongoing medical conditions herself, they are all doctor prescribed, and it's this difference that Louise thinks would concern her mother.

'I did tell two of my cousins while I was there though,' says Louise.

'One was amazing, the other one thought the jabs were dangerous, even though she is carrying some extra weight and suffers from arthritis, making exercise difficult, and it might be an option for her.'

Both cousins were however sworn to secrecy in order that Louise's mum doesn't find out.

Louise feels that the judgement and fear she has seen is unique to weight-loss medication.

'Nobody would ever question me taking blood pressure medication, and no one would suggest you just use willpower to stop smoking if you were using patches to help curb cravings.'

Another aspect of judgement that Louise has experienced is fielding questions about when she is going to stop losing weight. While she's lost 40 per cent of her starting weight, she still has weight she wants to drop. Her targets include being able to perform a lunge without pain in her knees, a reduction in her blood pressure and being in the right area of a healthy BMI score (Louise's BMI has gone from 57 to 33, which is still categorised as obese). But friends have a set idea of Louise and perhaps feel she is a bigger person naturally and so should remain 'big'.

Not discussing weight loss with those immediately around you can be an isolating experience. Louise does however have a supportive community.

'One of the reasons I chose Juniper for my weight-loss drugs is that it's not just like getting injections from a random online pharmacy. There's a whole program around it and a health coach to hand and with the Facebook community group you've got thousands of people on the same journey as you, cheering you on. I've had a lot of support, and I think that has made it easier.'

'Of course, people that are also using weight-loss jabs aren't going to judge you, because they are doing exactly the same thing. Regardless of whether they are there to lose two stone or a lot more.'

'And there's an unspoken agreement in the group that while people can see the icon from your Facebook profile when you comment in the group, you don't mention who you've seen to anyone else. And if you do feel uncomfortable about anyone you recognise seeing you, you can block them.'

'More recently I've become a mentor to those just starting out on their journey.'

'I haven't thought about when or if I will come off the drug yet as a still have a way to go. But I do know now that I enjoy cooking, whereas before I couldn't be bothered. I've developed a repertoire of healthy recipes, that are easy to make, that I can use for batch cooking. They go in the freezer and then if I'm busy and don't have time to cook, or I'm tired, there's something there. I make a proper balanced salad with protein and healthy fats that lasts for three days too.'

Louise suspects that there must be many women like herself who are using the weight-loss jabs but not sharing that they are.

'In this UK Facebook group there are 20,000 people, and the newer group that started in June had 1,500 members within a month. And this is just for Juniper. There are hundreds of suppliers out there. There are tens of thousands of people taking these drugs.'

CONCLUSION

In this book we've heard the stories of women from across the world. These women are different in age, race, cultural and religious background, educational attainment, sexual orientation and job and relationship status. But they have something in common; they all keep, or have kept, secrets. And their stories cut across generations and geographical boundaries, showing the experience of women keeping secrets is universal and has been ever-present.

So, why are women secret and secretive? Do they enjoy it? And do they do it by choice?

Perhaps the most obvious answer to the question of why women keep secrets is to protect themselves. Firstly, in a physical sense. Women often need to pass by unnoticed so that they can go about their daily life and their work; or practise their beliefs, politics and interests, without being a victim of violence, or the threat of violence. This is true for those speaking up against misogynistic and cruel regimes, those living with abuse and those whose professional lives may bring them into contact with danger and dangerous people.

Alongside physical safety, women are also subject to shame and judgement and so must keep quiet to protect their emotional and mental health too. Survivors of sexual, child and domestic abuse and assault and incest are all victims twice over, first at the hand of the abuser and then by cultural, societal and even judicial systems that ask why they didn't stop the abuse, why they didn't say 'no' and what they could have done differently. The narrative of 'He did it, she hid it' can be incredibly damaging in both the short and long term. Even women who own their romantic life and sexuality by enjoying love affairs, embracing their sexuality and making a living out of their own body, are shamed. The outside world polices their behaviour and acts as judge and jury.

And this shame and judgement apply not just to a woman's physical being. As beliefs and practices perhaps more typically associated with the feminine mind attract criticism, women may find themselves shamed for being too emotional or intuitive. Struggles with mental health and neurodiversity can also be vilified by a society that expects women to be in control for the sake of others: partners, children and other dependent relatives, and colleagues. Even women who decide to lose weight face stigmas associated with vanity and what society decides is 'proper' behaviour and a 'proper' size. A woman's body and mind can feel like they belong to society.

As well as protecting themselves, women also go about their lives with quiet discretion to protect their family and those they love, including pets and other animals, as well as their clients and even their country in times of conflict. Women may keep industry secrets to protect an art form such as magic that they have dedicated their working lives to, and to protect others who belong to societies with secrets they may wish to keep under wraps. Women retain a sense of duty to keep private the information that could otherwise damage others, not least the sex worker who is also the keeper of secrets on behalf of her clients.

Interestingly, many things associated with women are also kept secret in society. This includes women's bodies and how they work, menstruation, sexual pleasure, pregnancy, birth and menopause. When it comes to pain women are taught to suffer in silence from a young age: period cramps, endometriosis, painful sex and the trauma of childbirth and post-partum recovery, these things are often not openly discussed and sometimes dismissed by the medical profession. Scientology even encourages silent birth, suggesting minimal conversation while a woman labours, partly so that the child is not damaged by negative imprints or 'engrams' of the process. Sometimes the desires, passions and ambitions of women are also considered secondary, with women often only defined by their relation to others – mother, wife, mistress – the object rather than the subject in our language. Society may even require women to be modest and humble about their achievements in a way that men are not required to be.

Women are sometimes silent because of a lack of information and visible role models. They may not recognise abuse as such, if they have never been given the language and tools to identify it. And they may not know that their sexuality is not 'wrong' until they meet others who feel the same way they do.

Women may even be healing and bettering themselves in secret. They may seek out knowledge, therapies, activities and organisations where they can explore what else life could offer them, and how they could become better educated.

Women are also manipulated into silence by abusers, who seek only to protect themselves and by religious and cultural beliefs rooted in misogyny, where it is a woman's role to keep herself pure. Those regimes that would like to remove women from public life altogether know that talking between women could threaten their authority, and so they seek to silence and isolate women, preventing them from gathering, sharing stories, seeking advice and education from others, and from accessing medical and maternal care. Here silence brings with it fear and danger to life.

It seems that secrets can be a shield to protect us and those we care about, but also a weapon to be used against us.

And how exactly are women keeping their secrets? In most cases, women keep their lives hidden through silence. They have developed a skillset that includes being able to go about their day unnoticed and thus unquestioned and underestimated. They are not bold and visible and threatening. They do not seek confrontation. They may also compartmentalise their life, so that the secret and hidden parts of it remain in one area, with the other sections of their life are kept completely separate. Women may have a private life that is very different from their public one.

For some, keeping secrets enables them to do their work to the best of their ability and keep the confidence of others they have a duty to protect. But in other cases, silence often comes with isolation, and many women with secrets find themselves both lonely and alone. Without the benefit of support, they may feel unable to accept themselves, thus feel unlovable and unable to love

Keeping secrets is a complex act. It often requires weaving a web to hide behind, creating diversions and convincing stories to throw people off your trail. You might need an alibi or an alternative reality. This can be wearing over time and becomes a heavy load to carry by yourself. Hiding their experiences, good or bad, what they value and enjoy, or how they are or feel often comes at a personal cost to women. It may affect their mental health, and they may spiral into addictive behaviours. Silence can also collude with a perpetrator.

This is when the importance of other female confidants is often vital. Again, and again, the women I spoke to, have a few close female friends or relatives they can confide in, particularly when their secret involves love, sex and sexuality, or being a survivor of abuse; the areas in which women seem to be most judged. Here a supportive sisterhood comes into its own. The importance of judgement-free help, advice and support from those who understand and can be trusted cannot be underestimated.

What happens when women do speak up? For many of those I spoke to, breaking the silence afforded them healing and power. They felt better about themselves and were able to find others to empathise and others with similar experiences in life. If you are reading this and are yet to share your secret with others but want to, and it feels right to do so, ask for help. There are people out there prepared to support you and there are people like you.

But speaking out and up should be the decision of the woman herself and done only for her benefit, or unless she feels breaking her silence will help others and she is happy to do so. It must be on her terms, she must be ready to share, and she must feel safe to do so. When the time is right, a woman who wants to tell, needs places to go, people to listen and if necessary robust systems in place to support her, be they legal or practical.

The research interviews for this book were tremendously moving at times, speaking to women who have dealt and are still dealing with so much. They were however prepared to talk for the betterment of other women, which is a testament to their strength and the power of lived experience. They were bold and brave to step forward. And we should see them, thank them and respect them. Many of the women were skilled professionals, who are able to use elements of secrecy for justice, counselling and the emotional and erotic needs of others They are all making the world a better place for men and women.

But certain conversations must still happen. And these conversations should centre around why women are still shamed for the things abusers do to them, or for simply being themselves in a world that can be so unaccepting. In the words of Gisèle Pelicot, this shame 'isn't ours to feel'. We must also become comfortable with discussing topics such as consent, misogynistic porn and abuse with our children to empower them and to protect them. We must ask why our legal system is still letting women down again, and again, and what we can do to change that.

The advice I have gleaned from talking and listening to these dauntless women is 'never stop sharing when it is safe to do so, look for those who can help and those who can be helped. And, if you are told a secret, hold it and its owner safe.'

For those affected by any of the issues covered in this book, there is a comprehensive further resources section on the following pages. If you are fortunate enough not to need this support right now, consider volunteering or donating to these organisations, so they can continue to help women like those featured in this book.

FURTHER RESOURCES

If you've been affected by any of the issues covered in this book, or if you want to learn more about some of the ideas and organisations discussed, the list below will help direct you.

**If you are in immediate danger, call 999
Access free support at any time from
The Samaritans on 116 123**

Chapter 1
Afghanistan/women's rights:
Friends of Afghan Women Network (FAWN) https://www.friendsofafghanwomennetwork.co.uk
Seeks to empower Afghan women and girls by advancing their economic resilience, safeguarding their human rights, and promoting equitable access to education.
UN Women https://www.unwomen.org/en
UN Women is the UN organization delivering programmes, policies and standards that uphold women's human rights and ensure that every woman and girl lives up to their full potential.
Amnesty International https://www.amnesty.org/en/
A global movement of more than 10 million people who are committed to creating a future where human rights are enjoyed by everyone.
The Circle https://www.thecircle.ngo

A global feminist organisation, founded by Annie Lennox and other leading women, supporting women and girls confronting gender-based violence and economic inequality across the world.

Malala Fund https://malala.org

Working for a world where every girl can learn and choose her own future.

Chapter 2
Animal rights:

IAWPC International Animal Coalition https://iawpc.org

Consists of 27 respected international animal welfare and protection organisations from around the world, with extensive knowledge and expertise in these areas. Contact the IAWPC by sending a message to: +44 7784412108.

The Animal Protection Index https://api.worldanimalprotection.org

Produced by World Animal Protection, the index is a ranking of 50 countries around the globe according to their legislation and policy commitments to protecting animals.

Viva! https://viva.org.uk

The UK's leading vegan campaigning charity, specialising in undercover investigations and high-profile animal campaigns.

People for the Ethical Treatment of Animals (PETA) Foundation https://www.peta.org.uk

A UK-based charity dedicated to establishing and protecting the rights of all animals.

Hogwood: A Modern Horror Story – available on Netflix

Cowspiracy: The Sustainability Secret https://www.cowspiracy.com

A feature-length environmental documentary that reveals the devastating environmental impact large-scale factory farming has on our planet.

Chapter 3
Child sex abuse:
Childline – 0800 1111

A free, private and confidential service for anyone under 19 in the UK with any issue they're going through.

Don't Hold Back, by Emma Jane Taylor

A self-help book to encourage others to find their voice, and to give thought and process into the difficulties around CSA, rejection and abandonment.

Project 90-10 https://project9010.com

Set up to educate, raise awareness and protect against child sexual abuse. Home of the P.A.C.K. educational programmes, providing vital tools and information to safeguard children.

The Maggie Oliver Foundation https://www.themaggieoliverfoundation.com

Provides emotional support and legal advocacy to survivors of childhood sexual abuse and exploitation.

Lucy Faithful Foundation https://www.lucyfaithfull.org.uk

Support for anyone with a concern about child sexual abuse and its prevention.

Stop It Now https://www.stopitnow.org.uk

Anonymous helpline, email and chat services for anyone with concerns about child sexual abuse. Can help if you are worried about your own thoughts, feelings or behaviour, or with any concerns about another adult or young person.

Domestic Abuse:
Refuge https://refuge.org.uk

The largest specialist domestic abuse organisation in the UK.

The National Domestic Abuse Helpline 0808 2000 247

The 24-hour helpline is for women experiencing domestic abuse, their family, friends and others calling on their behalf. Individuals can set a codeword and send a message to the helpline to either contact them by phone or email. They can also contact an alternative number, such as a friend's phone.

The Men's Advice Line can be contacted on 0808 801 0327.

Woman's Aid https://www.womensaid.org.uk

The national charity working to end domestic abuse against women and children.

The Employers' Initiative on Domestic Abuse (EIDA) https://www.eida.org.uk

Supports over 2,000 large and small businesses, collectively comprising over 25 per cent of the UK workforce, to take effective action on domestic abuse.

Surviving Economic Abuse (SEA) https://survivingeconomicabuse.org

Taking vital steps towards a world where survivors can live their lives free from abuse and exploitation.

Hourglass https://wearehourglass.org/who-we-are

The Hourglass mission is simple: end the harm, abuse and exploitation of older people in the UK.

Chapter 4
Sexual Assault:

NHS advice: https://www.nhs.uk/live-well/sexual-health/help-after-rape-and-sexual-assault/

Sexual Assault Referral Centres (SARCs)

Located across the country and available for everyone, offering a range of services, including crisis care, medical and forensic examinations, emergency contraception and testing for STIs. They can also arrange access to an independent sexual violence advisor (ISVA), mental health support, sexual violence support services and reporting an assault to the police.

Rape Crisis https://rapecrisis.org.uk

Feminist charity working to end child sexual abuse, rape, sexual assault, sexual harassment and all other forms of sexual violence.

Safeline https://safeline.org.uk/about-us/

A specialist charity that works to prevent sexual abuse and support those affected to cope and recover.

Enough https://myenough.com

Not-for-profit providers of self-swab rape kits that can be used at home. Results belong only to the person who owns the kit.

Chapter 5
Wartime coding and Bombe machines:

Bletchley Park https://www.bletchleypark.org.uk

Backing Bletchley: The Codebreaking outstations from GCHQ, by Ronald Koorm

The Bletchley Girls: War, Secrecy, Love and Loss, by Tessa Dunlop

Codebreaker Girls: A Secret Life at Bletchley Park, by Jan Slimming

Chapter 6
Private investigators:

Jen Jarvie E: jen@crimeinstitute.co.uk Tel: 07796148635

Sarah Martin E: Sarah@sm-investigations.co.uk Tel: 020 3191 6666

Association of British Investigators https://www.theabi.org.uk

The largest directory of accredited professional investigators in the UK and members worldwide, who must meet rigorous membership standards.

Chapter 7
The Magic Circle and Freemasonry:

The Magic Circle https://themagiccircle.co.uk

Magic society with over 1,700 members worldwide brought together by a passion for magic.

The Order of Women's Freemasons https://www.owf.org.uk

The UK's oldest and largest Masonic organisation for women, works on the lines of regular male Freemasonry.

The Honourable Fraternity of Ancient Freemasons, Freemasonry for Women https://hfaf.org
Founded in 1913 for friendship, inspiration and empowerment.
Grande Loge Féminine de Belgique (GLFB) https://www.glfb-vglb.org
Formed in 1981 when four lodges that were previously part of the French Women's Masonic Union came together to form an autonomous organisation in Belgium.
Doneraile Court: The Story of the Lady Freemason, by Kathleen Aldworth Foster

Chapter 8
Adult content and sex work:
National Ugly Mugs (NUM) https://nationaluglymugs.org
UK-wide charity working with sex workers to do research, design and deliver safety tools and provide support services to people in adult industries.
Sex Workers Advocacy and Reistance Movement (SWARM) https://www.swarmcollective.org
A sex worker-led collective based in the UK. Advocates for the rights of everyone who sells sexual services.

Chapter 9
Lesbian lives:
LGBT Foundation https://lgbt.foundation
A national health and well-being charity where queer hope and joy flourish.
LGB Alliance https://lgballiance.org.uk
For lesbians, gay men and bisexuals to live free from discrimination or disadvantage based on their sexual orientation.
FFLAG https://www.fflag.org.uk
A national voluntary organisation and charity dedicated to supporting families and their LGBT+ loved ones.
No Place to Lie: Secrets Unlocked, a Promise Kept, by Helen Garlick

Chapter 10
Secret affairs:
Relate https://www.relate.org.uk

The largest provider of relationship support in England and Wales which help millions of people every year through individual and couples' relationship counselling.

National Family Mediation https://www.nfm.org.uk

Helps families in England and Wales resolve all the practical, legal, emotional and financial issues that arise from separation or divorce.

Chapter 11
Kink and fetish:
Dr Lori Beth Bisbey https://drloribethbisbey.com

Accredited Advanced Gender, Sex, Relationship Diversity Therapist (Pink Therapy), sex and intimacy coach, and registered psychologist.

Backlash https://www.backlash.org.uk

Set up to provide academic, legal, and campaigning resources to defend freedom of sexual expression.

Feminists Against Censorship https://www.facebook.com/groups/7169348275/

A network of women founded in 1989 in the United Kingdom to present the feminist arguments against censorship, particularly of sexual materials, and to defend individual sexual expression.

National Coalition for Sexual Freedom https://ncsfreedom.org

Committed to creating a political, legal and social environment in the US that advances equal rights for consenting adults who engage in alternative sexual and relationship expressions.

Chapter 12
Support for survivors of incest and childhood sexual abuse:
The National Association for People Abused in Childhood
Helpline - 0800 801 0331 https://napac.org.uk

The UK's only dedicated national support service for adult survivors of all forms of childhood abuse.

The Survivor's Trust https://thesurvivorstrust.org

An umbrella group of support services, search for one near you offering specialist rape and sexual abuse services.

Hypersexuality:

Sex and Love Addicts Anonymous (SLAA) https://slaauk.org

A Twelve Step, Twelve Tradition oriented Fellowship open to anyone who may have a problem with sex addiction, love addiction, romantic obsession, co-dependent relationships, fantasy addiction and/or sexual, social and emotional anorexia.

Sex Addicts Anonymous UK (SAA) https://saauk.info

A non-profit making social enterprise to help individuals to stop addictive and illegal sexual behaviours.

The Freedom of Information Act https://www.gov.uk/make-a-freedom-of-information-request

The Freedom of Information Act (FOIA) and Freedom of Information (Scotland) Act (FOISA) give you the right to see information. You can request information from some public authorities including government bodies, councils and schools as well as the NHS, the police force and publicly owned companies.

Chapter 13
Witchcraft and the Occult:

The Museum of Witchcraft: Objects, Practices, Symbols: A Guided Tour to the Occult, by Diane Purkiss

The Pagan Federation https://www.paganfed.org

Supports all Pagans to ensure they have the same rights as the followers of other beliefs and religions.

Chapter 14
Shamanism:

Shamanism: An Introduction, by Margaret Stutley

The Foundation for Shamanic Studies Europe https://www.shamanicstudies.co.uk

A UK non-profit offering shamanic trainings and workshops in person and online.

Earth Heart Shamanism UK https://shamanismuk.com

A source of Celtic Shamanism teachings offering Shamanism courses and workshops.

Chapter 15
ADHD/neurodivergence and mental health:

In a mental health crisis, **call 111** for urgent but non-life-threatening help or **call 999** if there is immediate danger to yourself or others.

You can also access the Shout Crisis Text Line (https://giveusashout.org) by texting 85258.

The Samaritans https://www.samaritans.org **Call 116 123**

The charity that prevents suicide through the power of human connection.

NeuroQueer: A Neurodivergent Guide to Love, Sex, and Everything in Between, by CJ DeBarra

Switchboard https://switchboard.lgbt

The national LGBTQIA+ support line.

ADHD & Women with Dr Anneka Tomlinson https://seedtalksacademy.co.uk/adhd-and-women

An on-demand course to give insight into ADHD in women, including how hormones and pregnancy can affect the condition.

Enhance the UK, changing society's view on disability https://enhancetheuk.org

The ADHD Foundation & Allied Neurodevelopmental Services https://www.adhdfoundation.org.uk

Offering support to those with neurodevelopmental conditions such as ADHD, Autism, Dyslexia, DCD, Dyscalculia, OCD and Tourette's Syndrome.

ADHD UK https://adhduk.co.uk

A charity whose mission is to help those affected by ADHD – either those who have the condition or people close to them: family, friends, employers, and co-workers.

Move With Emma https://www.movewithemma.co.uk

Personal trainer, devoted to women's health and fitness.

Chapter 16
Weight-loss jabs:

NHS weight loss guidance and free Weight Loss Plan app https://www.nhs.uk/better-health/lose-weight/

Juniper https://www.myjuniper.co.uk

Weight-loss drug provider.

Notes

Do you have any similar experiences to the Secret Women we speak to in this book? Feel free to use these next few pages to add your own thoughts or to write your own secret journal.

Notes

www.ingramcontent.com/pod-product-compliance
Lightning Source LLC
Chambersburg PA
CBHW052128030426
42337CB00028B/5073